Training for Service
in the
ADULT DEPARTMENT

by CHARLES R. GRESHAM

STANDARD PUBLISHING
Cincinnati, Ohio   3228

1966
STANDARD PUBLISHING
Cincinnati, Ohio
Printed in U.S.A.

PREFACE

The old adage, "You can't teach an old dog new tricks," was never really applicable. Adults have always been learning. Moses was eighty years old when he learned the most significant lesson of his life at Horeb. David was a mature adult when the prophet, Nathan, taught him the evils of covetousness and adultery. Saul of Tarsus was of mature years when he was confronted by the living Lord and taught by the Master Teacher.

It has only been in the twentieth century, however, that we have rediscovered what the Bible has always taught—persons are teachable at every age! Only in the past fifty years has the church been taking adult education seriously.

This book has been written to foster adult education in the church. It may be used in teacher-training classes or as individual study material. The average adult teacher was kept in mind as these chapters were written; hence, the practical emphasis is stressed throughout. On the other hand, it is hoped that there is enough philosophical and theoretical grounding contained in the work to satisfy those more advanced.

The purpose of the author will be accomplished if this book can but inspire and challenge the adult departments of our Bible schools to become more effective reaching and teaching instruments in the hands of the Master Teacher. May His Spirit—the Spirit of Truth who teaches us all—use this book to that end.

—CHARLES R. GRESHAM

CONTENTS

CHAPTER 1

You Are Never Too Old to Learn

It has only been in recent years that much emphasis has been placed upon adult education in our culture. There were several reasons for a lack of emphasis upon adult learning, but most basic was a failure to recognize what had been going on all the time. Lyceums, chautauquas, reading clubs, correspondence courses, and university extension work were all operative in the adult field; but not until the American Association for Adult Education began its work were these seen as a part of a continuing stream of educational emphasis flowing through adult life. It was in the third decade of this century that this discovery was made by both society and the church. Since that time, adult education has had a definite place in both secular and religious education.

What Is an Adult?

Before we can adequately discuss adult learning, we should first define adulthood. What is meant when one uses the term adult? Is chronological age the only criterion, or do other factors enter into our definition?

Chronologically, age twenty-five is generally accepted as the dividing line between later adolescence and early adulthood. However, from the standpoint of mental, social, and spiritual maturity this age is rather arbitrary. In our present culture, there are forces that so mold individual persons as to develop maturity much earlier than in past eras. On the other hand, there are other forces that will tend to deter maturity in some individuals. Because of this, chronological age cannot be the only factor considered in defining adulthood.

The basic factor that makes for adulthood is maturity. Physical maturity, generally achieved by age twenty-five, is one characteristic of adulthood, but only one. Mental, social, and moral maturity are also characteristics. Such maturity involves independence and responsibility. One may be considered an adult who is relatively independent of parents and who has taken his place in society as a responsible person, responsible for his own behavior and responsible to his society (community and church) to make some contribution to its well-being.

In defining adulthood, then, such things as chronological age, mental age, emotional maturity, economic self-support, moral responsibility, and independence of parental control must be taken into consideration.

Adults Can Learn!

Not too many years ago it was commonly believed that adults had lost their power to learn. Such an authority as William James (in 1893) had given his judgment that "outside of their own business, the ideas gained by men before they are twenty-five are practically the only ideas that they shall have in their lives. They cannot get anything new. Disinterested curiosity is past, the mental grooves and channels set, the power of assimilation gone. Whatever individual exceptions might be cited, these are soil to prove the rule."[1]

More recent research has shown that this conception was quite mythical and did not square with reality. The psychologist, E. L. Thorndike, made a study of the ability of adults to learn. The results of his research were published in 1920 under the title, *Adult Learning.* His conclusion was that all adults can learn; in all probability, they can learn all that they need to learn. He stated further that no one under forty-five should restrain himself from trying to learn anything because of a belief or a fear that he is too old to be able to learn. Irving Lorge has continued Thorndike's pioneering work and his results show quite positively the possibility of excellent learning by those of adult age.

Another experiment in adult learning was conducted shortly after World War I by using the Army Alpha Test on all members of families in nineteen villages of Massachusetts, New Hampshire, and Vermont. The results indicated that learning ability reaches its peak between the ages of 18 and 21. A decline follows that is much more gradual than the curve of growth, but which by the age of 55 involves a secession to the 14-year level. The chart on page 9 from *Psychological Studies of Human Development* (New York, 1952) gives a visual picture of the conclusion of this experiment.

Later studies have been made, but these all indicate that age has no veto power over learning. Naturally, such factors as education, motivation, and interest will cause some variation in adult aptitude in learning experience; but, as Kidd says, "Increasingly evidence is coming in to support the view that adults of all ages can learn effectively."[2] The old adage needs to read: "Give me a child until he is *seventy* and I care not who has him in charge after that!"

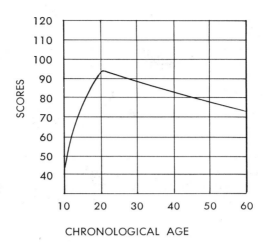

CHRONOLOGICAL AGE

Adults Are Important

Too often, in our emphasis upon young life, its nature and Christian nurture, we tend to overlook our adults. This is particularly true in the educational program of the church. Although the Sunday-school movement began some two hundred years ago as a movement directed primarily toward children, we cannot in the twentieth century place all our emphasis in religious education upon children and youth. Adults are important too!

The Bible, our textbook, is an adult book, written by adults to adults. Though it exalts childhood as no other book, its message of redemption centers around adult life. God revealed himself and His will to Abraham, Isaac, Jacob, Moses, and the prophets after they had come into adult years. The early church, sent forth into a hostile world with this life-giving message of a personal Saviour and Lord, was directed by Spirit-filled apostles and prophets—adults. The qualifications of bishops or elders and deacons, to whom were committed the spiritual oversight of succeeding generations of Christians, are adult qualifications. Such evidence certainly points to the significance of adult life in God's plan and program as revealed in the Scriptures.

Christian history testifies to the same truth. Adults are important! It is always an adult through whom the Holy Spirit initiates reform or advance in Christendom. Luther's stand against Romish practice and his emphasis upon the Scriptural doctrines of justification by faith and the priesthood of every believer came as a result of mature adult study, meditation, and prayer. The reaction of Wesleyan fervent evangelicalism to a stultifying formalism within the Church of England was a product of adult insight. The Campbells (father and son), Walter Scott, Barton W. Stone, Isaac Errett, and other first and second generation leaders of the Restoration movement were all adults when they caught the vision of a united church committed to the simple faith and practice of the New Testament. Through adults God has moved and accomplished His purposes in succeeding generations of Christian history. Adults are important!

Adults are important in our local churches. They constitute the backbone of our congregations. Adults provide the leadership of every area of congregational life; adults provide the finances by which the congregation's program at home and abroad is carried out. Without adults our local churches would be leaderless, impotent, financially insecure, and in danger of extinction. Adults are important!

Since adults are so essential to every area of church life and since they have the ability to learn as long as they live, it is important that local churches provide every opportunity possible for adult growth and nurture in the Christian faith. They need knowledge of the faith, skill in communicating it to others, and the development of those Christian attitudes that are so essential in making them winsome and lovely Christian persons. Let's face it. Some Christian characteristics take a long time to develop. If these are not obtained by adulthood, the development must continue into adulthood.

Every local congregation has the responsibility to provide learning opportunities in these three areas for every adult involved in any way with the program of the local church. Why? Because adults are important and one is never too old to learn!

Books for Further Study

CLEMMONS, ROBERT S. *Dynamics of Christian Adult Education.* New York: Abingdon Press, 1958.
DOBBINS, G. S. *Understanding Adults.* Nashville: Convention Press, 1957.
GORHAM, DONALD. *Understanding Adults.* Philadelphia: Judson Press, 1948.
KIDD, J. R. *How Adults Learn.* New York: Association Press, 1959.
THORNDIKE, E. L. *Adult Learning.* New York: Macmillan Company, 1928.

Questions for Discussion

1. When may one be considered an adult? What is the basic factor of adulthood?

2. What have recent surveys shown about an adult's ability to learn?

3. What three factors enter into the degree to which adults learn?

4. Give three examples of how God has used adults in the development of His plans.

5. Why is it so important for the adults of the local church to be well informed?

NOTES

[1] William James, *Principles of Psychology* (2 vols.; Magnolia, Massachusetts: Peter Smith, Publisher).

[2] J. R. Kidd, *How Adults Learn* (New York: Association Press, 1959), p. 90. Used by permission.

CHAPTER 2

The Church School and Adults

What Is the Church School?

That which is known as the church school has developed historically from the "secular" Sunday school originated in 1780 by Robert Raikes in Gloucester, England. Originally, the Sunday school was conceived of as an instrument for providing general education (hence the word "secular") for poor children who had only Sunday as respite from work in the shops and factories of England. Raikes's experiment proved successful and swept like wildlife over Great Britain. Societies and unions were formed to provide promotion, funds, and teaching aids for these Sunday schools.

It was in America, however, that the Sunday-school idea made its greatest impact. Imported to America about 1785, the Sunday school fitted admirably into the "scheme of things" in this new republic. Since the principle of the separation of church and state was enunciated clearly in the Constitution, educators saw the impossibility of the state sponsoring religious education. As the public schools became more secular, the Sunday school became the instrument of the church to provide religious instruction for its youth.

By 1870 the Sunday school had become the major educational agency of the church. Interdenominational agencies such as the American Sunday School Union and the International Sunday School Convention had successfully promoted the Sunday-school idea so that all major religious communions recognized the educational value of the Sunday school. As a result of the efforts of these interdenominational institutions, mission Sunday schools came into existence on the American frontier often before churches were organized. Not only were these agencies concerned with promotion, they also provided guidance and supervision through a convention system developing from the county level up to the International Convention which met each four years.

With such guidance, the churches began to attempt to meet the educational needs of all the people in the church. In doing so, new organizations, agencies, and groups within the local church were developed. To the Sunday school were added youth programs (The

Society of Christian Endeavor being founded in 1881), Daily Vacation Bible School, weekday religious education, summer camps, and other such agencies as needs were seen and met. By the beginning of the second decade of this century, the educational program of local churches was often a hodge-podge of overlapping, often independent agencies, each going its own merry way. More mature educators saw that this was detrimental to the church since it did not suggest a unified and correlated educational program.

A committee was appointed by the Religious Education Association (an association of religious educators concerned with upgrading religious teaching by applying the educational idea) to study this need for correlation and unification of these varied intrachurch agencies. In 1913 this committee authorized the publication of a book, *The Church School*, by the chairman, W. S. Athearn. This book coined the term church school. Since then this term has proved most satisfactory and has supplanted other names such as Sunday school or Bible school. Dr. J. D. Murch says:

> *Church school* places the emphasis where it belongs. The church is responsible for the educational program. The New Testament recognizes no educational function apart from the *church*. The *church-school* program is inclusive of days, textbooks, and everything else involved in the educational task. The term *church school* expresses the idea that the church is functioning educationally. It is the most Scriptural, logical, comprehensive, and satisfying name. [1]

The implications involved in the use of the term *church school* are apparent. When we speak of adults in the church school we are attempting to see the total structure which the church provides for adult education. Our concern will not be with the Sunday morning Bible school alone, but with every other church program in which the educational ideal is to be found.

Growth of Interest in Adult Participation

Just as there has been a growing interest in general adult education, so there is a growing interest in adults participating in the church school. No longer is the church school conceived of as a child-training agency. Adults are recognizing that they need to grow in knowledge and skill as well. More and more adults themselves are demanding that the church provide learning experiences for them, for these adults assume responsibility in the church's ministry to its members and its community; they find that they need more knowledge and greater skills in order that they may serve in a competent manner.

History of the Adult Class Emphasis

Historically, the first concerted effort to emphasize adult Bible study was made by Marshall A. Hudson, a Baptist layman of Syracuse, New York. Hudson was "concerned about the need for Bible study by the young adult men in his community,"[2] so he organized a Bible class in which more than one hundred men were enrolled. The name "Baraca" was chosen as a class name. This success inspired Hudson's daughter to begin a class for women. This class adopted the name "Philathea" as a class designation. Thus, the Baraca-Philathea Bible Class movement was born.

This movement was interdenominational and succeeded in publicizing and promoting adult Bible-study classes in various religious groups throughout the nation. Its weakness was its stress on large crowds, competition, entertainment, and promotional schemes. It also tended to emphasize the independence and autonomy of the adult class, which created problems for a church-centered program of education. John T. Sizemore's analysis of this movement, from the Southern Baptist standpoint, is good.

> Probably no other group gave as much support to the Baraca-Philathea movement as did Southern Baptists during its early stages. Through it they enrolled thousands of men and women in Bible study. However, the paying of dues, the taking of orders from outside agencies, the development of unwholesome independence by the classes, and the extreme insistence on inspiration and entertainment—these factors were too much for church-minded Southern Baptists. [3]

In more recent years, due to the insistence of leading educators, adult classes have become an integral part or department of the Sunday morning Bible school, functioning not as independent entities but as a unit of a church-centered, Christian educational program.

Other Adult Phases of the Church School

If the church school (as has been defined) is to unify the total church educational program, then we must classify such extra adult educational features as men's and women's groups, training programs, fellowship groups, prayer cells, and prayer breakfasts within the adult church-school program. If this is not done, much duplication, competition, and inefficiency will result. Once such unification has taken place, then a correlation of all these educational agencies can be accomplished through a committee or board of education, authorized by the local church eldership and including in its membership representatives from all these educational organizations.

In larger churches where more groups, organizations, and departments would be involved, it might be necessary to have, in addition to the general committee on Christian education, cabinets for adult education, for youth education, and for childhood education. Thus, the general committee would act upon the recommendations and programs suggested by these age-group cabinets. In this way the general committee on Christian education would not become so unwieldy or get bogged down in a lot of unnecessary detail work that could be handled by these cabinets.

Problems in Adult Work[4]

One cannot discuss the place of adults in the church school without facing general problems in adult Christian education. Some of these are carry-overs from the traditions of the past; others come from the constant changes involved in contemporary society; still others seem to arise out of the failure of local congregations to meet ideally the needs of adults in a changing world. Whatever their source, these problems must be faced and some solutions attempted.

1. *The problem of grading.* Problems of grading are most prevalent in the adult area. Children and youth move from class to class, department to department, without any grave difficulties, but this is not true of adults. Some educational leaders (and total denominations) believe that grading by age and sex is done in the children and youth areas ought to prevail in the adult area as well. Others are as thoroughly convinced that a *functional grading* is best. Westphal says: "Our point of view is that the most satisfactory, and most logical, basis of grouping is *functional grouping,* a grouping in which adults grade themselves, not on an age basis, but on the basis of interest and needs."[5] Arguments can be produced for both viewpoints; therefore, it is impossible to be dogmatic at this point.

Perhaps a compromise could be suggested which would take into consideration the advantages of both types of grading. In the Sunday morning Bible school and evening training program, age-grouping could be generally followed with a few elective classes being offered for the benefit of those whose interests and needs are such as to cause them to react to or break away from the normal age-grouping which is generally followed. In men's and women's group meetings both age-grouping and interest-grouping will find a place as certain age groups tend to gravitate toward one another, and those with like interests seek each other out in informal study and fellowship groups. Then, both the educational and social values and functions of adult groups will be promoted and guaranteed. At any rate, hard and fast rules which would maintain either viewpoint ought to be avoided.

2. *The problem of enlisting men.* In many churches the basic adult problem (and, perhaps, the total church problem) is that of unenlisted men. The importance of men in the work of the church is quite apparent, yet there are frequently fewer men in our churches than women or children. As Dr. Sizemore points out: "When men are enlisted, whole families are reached, Christian homes are readily established, leadership is found and developed, church finances are no longer a problem, evangelism is greatly accelerated, and God is glorified!" [6]

What practical steps can be taken in reaching men? (1) More classes should be started. Better organization and correlation of men's work generally could be accomplished. The day of the large men's Bible class, often independent of the Bible school, appears to be over. Although it may have been successful in the 1920's it is no longer usually practical. (2) Men should be encouraged to enlist men. A regular program of visitation can be augmented by "Fisherman's Clubs," "Andrew Societies," organized "Man Hunts," and other special programs and campaigns of a similar nature. (3) Men who are enlisted should be put to work. Smaller classes and departments provide more opportunities for service, as men become class officers and, with proper training, teachers and leaders in the church school. Remember that your newly-enlisted people are generally more eager to work, so involve them in various activities while this enthusiasm is still there.

3. *The problem of single adults.* Though not as common as some of the other problems discussed in this chapter, the problem of single adults will have to be faced by a growing number of churches. In many instances no provision is made for the single adult as far as classes and programs of study are concerned. Often these adults who are unmarried feel out of place in both young married peoples classes and older adult classes graded according to sex, since their interests and needs are different. If possible, classes in the Sunday morning Bible school and special interest clubs and fellowship groups should be created for these neglected and often ignored people. In smaller churches this may be impossible; if so, personal help and counsel by educational and pastoral leaders may prove an adequate substitute.

4. *The problem of unenrolled church members.* Invariably, in every local church there are large numbers of church members who are not enrolled nor actively participating in the educational program of the church. These people are not only missing a great op-

16

portunity of growing in grace and knowledge through fellowship and learning, they may also be a detriment to the church through the examples they set for others. These people, if activated, could be a source of both spiritual and numerical power. In reaching these people the same methods and procedures should be followed as those used for enlisting non-Christians. Of course, there will be active members of our churches who do not participate in adult education opportunities, but who are active in worship, financial support, and other phases of church life. Special attention should be given to these people as the need for Bible study and Christian growth are presented tactfully, lovingly, and persistently.

5. *The problem of space and equipment.* Adult education through the church school can be carried out more effectively when proper equipment and adequate space are provided. Space for both departmental assemblies and individual classrooms should be provided. Comfortable chairs should be arranged in a manner conducive to member participation. To promote better educational procedures, classes should be limited to not more than twenty-five or thirty persons. Proper provision should be made for an adequate number of adult classrooms. Pictures, maps, chalkboards, usual visual aid equipment, and other such helps should be provided. Besides classrooms, parlors, recreational areas, and other such areas need to be reserved for adults. They need recreational, social, and fellowship activities just as the young people need them. In planning for new educational facilities, architectural services and source books such as *Planning Better Church Buildings* by William A. Harrell (Broadman Press), *Building and Equipping for Christian Education* by C. Harry Atkinson (National Council of the Churches of Christ in the U.S.A.), and *Protestant Church Building* by William Leach (Abingdon-Cokesbury Press) should be consulted.

Sometimes these problems may seem insurmountable, but remember that the solution to every problem presents a corresponding opportunity. These problems should challenge us to greater endeavor to improve the program of adult education through the church school.

Books for Further Study

Jones, Idris W. *Our Church Plans for Adult Education.* Philadelphia: Judson Press.

Murch, James DeForest. *Christian Education and the Local Church* (rev. ed.). Cincinnati: Standard Publishing, 1958.

Sizemore, John T. *The Sunday School Ministry to Adults.* Nashville: Convention Press, 1959.

WESTPHAL, EDWARD P. *The Church's Opportunity in Adult Education.*
Philadelphia: Westminster Press, 1941.

Questions for Discussion

1. Give a brief history of the development of the church school.

2. Why may the name church school be considered as an appropriate name?

3. Where and by whom was the Baraca-Philathea Bible Class movement begun?

4. Name several ways of grading or grouping adults.

5. Give three suggestions for enlisting more men in the Adult Department.

6. What are some of the problems the unenrolled church member creates for the church and for himself?

7. Describe a well-equipped adult Bible-school classroom.

8. Explain why careful attention should be given to building an effective Adult Department in the Bible school.

NOTES

[1] James DeForest Murch, *Christian Education and the Local Church* (rev. ed.; Cincinnati: Standard Publishing, 1958), footnote p. 165.

[2] John T. Sizemore, *The Sunday School Ministry to Adults* (Nashville: Convention Press, 1959), p. 15.

[3] *Ibid.*, p. 16.

[4] In this section I am indebted to ideas supplied by J. T. Sizemore, *op. cit.*, p. 45 ff.

[5] *Op. cit.*, p. 101.

[6] *Op. cit.*, p. 52.

CHAPTER 3

How to Understand Young Adults

In order to work with adults within the framework of the local church, it is necessary for leaders to understand something of the nature and needs of adulthood. We must come to a reasonably complete understanding of their problems, their interests, their backgrounds, their basic psychology and philosophy, and their consuming interests in life. General characteristics such as responsibility, independence, and physical and emotional maturity are apparent in adult life. Other characteristics can be seen as a more thorough study is made of the adult years. In order to make such a thorough study, the adult span of life must be divided into major cycles or areas. These major areas of adult life are young adulthood, middle adulthood ("the middle years"), older or later adulthood, and senior citizenship or retirement. Each area has its basic psychology, interests, and problems. The following chart, developed by Paul F. Douglass, indicates this: [1]

PERIOD	PROBLEM

Young Adulthood—
School to marriage
	Transition from organized school life, home protection, and adolescent friendships to adult world of lifework and individual responsibility. Concern for:
	  a. vocational skill
	  b. advancement
	  c. marriage and own home

Middle Years— Marriage to the children's marriages	Establishment of family and home, prestige status in community, vocational prestige, circle of friendships, development and advancement of children.
Free Years— Children leaving home to retirement	Interest in children's homes and grandchildren; general economic security, free time.
Senior Citizenship— From retirement	Engagement in purposeful and happy associations; comfort.

Characteristics of Early Adulthood

The age limits of early adulthood have generally been set from 25 to 35. This is somewhat arbitrary since many enter the adult category long before they reach the age of 25.

As soon as we begin to assign limitations to our early adult period we meet with problems. Some questions at this point will help us to see some of these problems. What will we do with the sixteen- or eighteen-year-olds who are married and still in school? How about the thirty-three-year-old who is still living at home? Is a thirty-five-year-old bachelor a "young" adult? Is the sixteen-year-old girl who is completely self-supporting a young "adult"? What of the circumstances where one of the marriage partners is substantially older than the other? These and other questions show how difficult it is to arrive at an adequate conception of young adulthood.

The change from late adolescence to early adulthood is generally one of crisis. As Charters indicates:

The transition from childhood to adulthood is perhaps the most complete and sudden crisis in life. The adult must try to earn a living at whatever job he can find, or in the way he considers right in his profession. He now has full responsibility for managing his own life. His mother and father do not arrange his marriage; this he does absolutely without guidance, even without any hints concerning the most fundamental and elementary facts of marriage and sex relations. He establishes his home, conducts his family life, rears his children. He finds his job and takes over adult business and civic duties. From the life of memorizing, idealizing, accepting dicta, he purges headlong into the life of learning and doing. [2]

Some of the basic characteristics of early adulthood are:

1. *Independence.* One of the most easily observable factors about the person approaching maturity is the desire to assume full responsibility for life. Of course, this desire may be based more upon the cultural demands of the present society than upon the recognition of the inner need. The young adult may not realize the full implications of why he *must* mature, but he will be anxious to assume the load because he knows people expect it of him.

Independence brings with it problems of both personal and impersonal nature. Adjustment to in-laws is one of the most prominent of the personal problems. Evelyn Duvall testifies:

The members of the younger generation are eager to become independent adults. They want to make their own mistakes and live their own lives without the hovering mother figure with her good or bad advice. They manifest a tremendous desire for maturity and for autonomy. The evidence that they are struggling for maturity is apparent in the intensity of their emotional reactions to the interest and help that mother-in-law gives them. [3]

Other problems, such as financial security, are of a more personal nature, yet just as real. All such problems indicate that independence of parents and previously-accepted authority involve corresponding responsibilities.

2. *Responsibility*. The assumption of expected responsibility makes the turning point from childhood to adulthood. This is a symbol of maturity. Responsibility may well be seen as the opposite side of the coin—independence. Independence involves responsibility; those who desire independence without accepting responsibility cannot be considered "adult" in the truest sense.

Responsibility develops gradually. Little does the late adolescent realize all that will be involved in becoming a man or woman, in choosing a mate, getting married, becoming a father or mother, and all the rest. Young people can never fully know the complications of these interrelated roles until they have actually experienced them. The manner and attitude with which young people attain these roles will indicate their maturity.

3. *Physical maturity*. The attainment of physical maturity is characteristic of the young adult age. Both physical and mental growth reach their apex in this period. Health is at the optimum. The sexual drive reaches its fruition in marriage and mature, adult love. There is a physical, mental, and emotional zest during these years never to be experienced fully again. It is in this period that our dreams begin to produce realities.

4. *Adaptability*. This is easily one of the most outstanding of the early adult's characteristics. While previous stages of development have seen more versatility in becoming adapted, yet this is adaptability utilized by adult reasoning. Because of this capacity these young adults become prime material for the church to utilize. Here is where leadership training should really begin.

5. *Confidence*. Perhaps no one would question the assertion that this period is the one in which more self-assurance and confidence is expressed than at any other. In some instances it is the fledgling leaving the nest with the supreme confidence of the inexperienced. In other cases it is the carefully coached prodigy of accomplishment who has not yet tasted the bitter pill of failure. In between these extremes fall all the rest of the group whose confidence will vary according to personality, but in whom confidence is a crowning factor.

Out of this confidence comes the ability to face overwhelming obstacles and conquer. What older people would consider impractical to undertake, these young adults will accept as a form of personal challenge to ingenuity and endurance. Church leaders can build upon such confidence as they challenge young adults to sacrificial service in the Master's kingdom.

6. *Orderliness.* While some of the techniques of the young adult may seem to approach the bizarre or brazen, yet in the total scheme of living he desires orderliness rather than chaos. The loose-jointedness of adolescence is as quickly rejected as is the tyrannical leadership of old age. Learning during this period is different too. Young adults are no longer interested in theory alone; they are primarily concerned with practical experience.

In this frame of reference the leader of young adults will be faced with the necessity of dealing with every situation reasonably, maturely, and cooperatively. Suggestions must be logical or they will not be considered as worthy. Young adults must be approached cooperatively or they will feel as though they are being coerced rather than guided.

The Needs of Young Adults

Young adults have basic needs and face specific problems. Such needs as the need to be a part of a participating group, the need of approval and love, the need of being accepted, and the need for security arise out of his psycho-social makeup. Other needs, more related to the religious life, are "the need to grow in freedom, the need for a sense of belonging, the need to become involved with other persons, the need to understand life's deeper meanings, the need to cooperate in creativity, and the need to experience relatedness to God."[4] Of course, these needs are to be found in all adults, but it is in the early adult period that these needs must be recognized and provided for.

In recent years, Robert J. Havighurst has suggested that each period of human growth development has certain "developmental tasks" that must be handled correctly if proper orientation is to result. He defines these as tasks that arise "out of a certain period in the life of an individual, successful achievement of which leads to his happiness and to success with later tasks, while failure leads to unhappiness in the individual, disapproval by the society, and difficulty with later tasks."[5]

The developmental tasks of early adulthood are crucial. If properly handled, the period is full of rich opportunities of creative growth and accomplishment. If improperly handled, young adulthood can become sterile, arid, and selfish. Dr. Havighurst says: "Early adulthood is the most individualistic period of life and the loneliest one, in the sense that the individual, or, at the most, two individuals, must proceed with a minimum of social attention and assistance to tackle the most important tasks of life." [6]

What are these developmental tasks that each young adult must face?

1. *The young adult must find a vocation that will support him economically and will satisfy him mentally, emotionally, and morally.* Consciously or unconsciously, each person expects that his work will satisfy needs and desires that lie deeper than mere economics. "Die Arbeit macht das Leben süss," says the proverb: "It is work which makes life sweet."

This task may not be as easy as it appears. Today, the increasing complexity of technology has created an enormous number of different jobs. Almost all of these require special training, some long years of arduous education. The temperament or personality of the individual will also be a determining factor. Therefore, self-knowledge, education, and planning all enter into this task.

2. *The young adult must develop a mature relationship with a marriage partner.* Not only must a suitable mate be selected, responsibility and mutual aid must be assumed in the marriage relationship. This is no easy task! It involves willingness on the part of each partner to understanding and continuous growth. The Truebloods state it well:

> The commitment which we call marriage is not a bargain! It is a situation in which each gives all that he has, including all his devotion and all the fruits of his toil . . . The result is that marriage is an amazing relation in which the ordinary rules of business, with its contracts and escape clauses and limited liabilities, are despised and set aside. Marriage is not marriage at all if it is conditional or with the fingers crossed. [7]

Only where mature love is foundational will a proper relationship be created. Such love cements two partners together into a bond that defies all the forces within society seeking to disintegrate this basic, God-given partnership.

Young adults must be educated adequately to assume marriage responsibility. Clemens suggests that there are a number of factors involved in marriage education, since marriage has theological, sociological, psychological, physiological, recreational, economical, and legal relationships. [8] Some of these only the church can adequately treat; therefore, the church has a responsibility in helping young people to see these relationships involved in marriage.

3. *The young adult must assume the role of a parent.* This is a major crisis in life, yet one that leads to further growth and maturity. When that first child comes, it may be an entering wedge sep-

23

arating rather than uniting the young couple. The new baby may become the total object of affection and parents may forget their responsibilities to each other. Or the sudden responsibility may overwhelm the young mother, making her feel inadequate, insecure, and afraid.

Fellowship groups within the church's life can aid young parents in preparing for parenthood. Here, with proper guidance and in a permissive atmosphere, young adults can explore their needs and problems in the light of Biblical injunctions and common sense.

4. *Young adults must learn to accept social responsibility.* Young adults are so busy getting started in a vocation, beginning a home, and becoming parents that they often forget that they must share in the responsibility of and make contribution to the society of which they are a part. Every Christian must be a good citizen, assuming his role in political and community tasks. There are community needs that must be met by the cooperation of adults.

The church should make special effort to educate young adults to their common task as citizens, and, if possible, interest young adult groups in special projects that will benefit community life.

5. *Young adults must establish a deep, personal faith.* No longer are there parents to turn to when troubles, disappointments, and doubts arise. There is need for a sure faith that can stand the testing that increased responsibility involves. A growing faith in the living God, greater understanding of the redemptive work of Christ, and a greater dependence upon the Holy Spirit come only as the young adult is committed to the life and work of the church.

6. *Young adults must face certain specific problems.* If not properly and adequately handled, they can ruin life, or at least keep the young adult from developing into the kind of personality pleasing to God.

7. *Changing interests often create problems for young adults.* In studies made by Edward K. Strong, Jr.,[9] and E. L. Thorndike[10] it was found that at least fifty percent of the changes in interests occurred between the ages of twenty-five and thirty-five. This fact in itself bodes neither good nor evil. There are possibilities of good in that this suggests that young adults are flexible and, through proper guidance, can be led to develop new interests more beneficial to the growth of their spiritual lives. On the other hand, this same fact suggests that this period can produce a change of interest that will prove harmful. To develop interests that will develop physically, challenge mentally, and uplift spiritually is a great need of this age.

24

8. *Often the young adult is faced with the problem of religious doubt.* As the reflective element of the intellect becomes more and more pronounced, more attention is given to the systematic and logical consistency of religious beliefs. Young adults, particularly those with college education, desire to develop a Christian philosophy of life consistent with facts and experience. They want to see things in proper perspective and universal relationships. They attempt to establish standards for thinking and acting, and they are eager to evaluate experience in light of these standards.

Out of such desires doubts often arise. The young adult leader should attempt to meet these doubts without sidestepping them or ignoring them. They are real to the young adult, and a stronger faith awaits their solution. Working together in an intellectually honest, yet God-directed atmosphere, solutions and answers can be found.

9. *A very real problem facing young adults arises out of their desire to build Christian homes.* Conscientious young adults recognize their responsibility in rearing their children in "the nurture and admonition of the Lord" (Ephesians 6:4). Too often, however, no practical guidance is given. Teachers and leaders of young adults must not take too much for granted. Specific step-by-step instructions with regard to developing family worship, pervading the home with a religious atmosphere, and providing Christian education in the home need to be given. Parent-teacher conferences will be helpful in gaining cooperation from parents so that the learning activity in the Nursery, Preschool, and Primary Departments on Sunday morning will be reinforced throughout the week. Take-home papers and religious journals should be utilized to the fullest extent. The building of a home library of wholesome Christian books will also aid measurably.

10. *Threatening to the true selfhood of young adults (and older adults as well) is the constant appeal to conformity.* In this modern age of uprootedness and mobility, of speed and mass communication, security is sought in conforming to those around us. Desire for status may easily replace the desire for inner growth and creative development. "Hidden persuaders" tend to destroy individual initiative and cause young adults to exchange higher values for material luxury and pleasure. Young adults must be urged to resist the damning blight of the "cult of conformity." They must be led to see the Christian emphasis on individual responsibility and initiative. Individual creativity, not mass conformity, must be presented to young adults as the goal toward which the self must strive!

What Young Adults Can Be

Young adults can be dynamic, growing persons! By "person" we mean

man as God intended him to be. Such a person knows that he is created by God to live in harmony with Him and his universe. He feels that he is in some measure fulfilling the destiny for which he was created. He is not free from the problems of his world, but he is able to use these problems for his own growth. He seeks to find himself and his place in a world of widening relationships and new factors in the culture. These factors threaten him, but they also present to him unequaled challenges and opportunities for personal growth.[11]

Young adults must be led, therefore, to develop strong physical bodies and sound mental health. When good mental health is present these results follow: (1) Young adults feel comfortable about themselves. They are not bowled over by their own emotions (fear, anger, love, jealousy, worry). They can take life's disappointments in stride. They can laugh at themselves. They can accept their own limitations and evaluate their own abilities realistically. They have self-respect. (2) They feel right about other people. They are able to enter into personal relationships that are satisfying and lasting. They assume their role within group life, accepting their responsibilities to their neighbors and fellowmen. They are able to give and receive love and affection. They respect the differences that they meet in others. (3) They are able to meet the demands of life. They do something about the problems that arise. They attempt to shape their environment when possible; they make the necessary adjustments when not possible. They welcome new ideas and experiences. They set realistic goals and plan ahead to meet them. They think for themselves and make their own decisions. They put their best effort into what they do and get satisfaction out of doing it. [12]

Above all, young adults must be challenged to develop spiritual attitudes toward life and to grow into Christlike character. A deep-seated interest in Christ and the church must be developed during this age period (if not already developed) so that their lives may be directed by Christian principles and given to sacrificial service. In this way young adults will become the growing, dynamic Christian persons God intended them to be.

Books for Further Study

CALDWELL, IRENE S. *Responsible Adults in the Church School Program.* Anderson, Indiana: Warner Press, 1961.

CHARTERS, LESLIE A. *Young Adults and the Church.* New York: Abingdon-Cokesbury Press, 1936.

CHAMBERLAIN, J. GORDON. *The Church and Its Young Adults.* New York: Abingdon-Cokesbury Press, 1943.

FRANKLIN, LOTTIE. *So You Work With Young Adults.* Anderson, Indiana: Warner Press, 1960.

GLEASON, GEORGE. *Single Young Adults in the Church.* New York: Association Press, 1952.

KERR, CLARENCE W. *God's Pattern for the Home.* Los Angeles: Cowman Publications, Inc., 1953.

TRUEBLOOD, ELTON AND PAULINE. *The Recovery of Family Life.* New York: Harper & Brothers, 1953.

Questions for Discussion

1. What are the three major cycles into which we divide adults?

2. What are the usual age limits for young adults?

3. List the six characteristics of young adults.

4. Why is leadership training important for young adults?

5. How may the characteristic of confidence be harnessed to improve the total program of the church?

6. What type of vocational guidance should the church give young adults?

7. Outline a program the church may follow in assisting young adults to establish Christian homes.

8. Discuss the importance of young adults in the church assuming the role of active citizens in the community.

9. What responsibility has the church toward her young adults in regard to answering religious doubts?

10. Describe a young adult who has reached emotional Christian maturity.

NOTES

[1] Paul F. Douglass, *The Group Workshop Way in the Church* (New York: Association Press, 1956), p. 117.

[2] Leslie A. Charters, *Young Adults and the Church* (New York: Abingdon-Cokesbury Press, 1936), p. 19.

[3] Evelyn Mills Duvall, *In-laws: Pro and Con* (New York: Association Press, 1954), pp. 297, 298.

[4] Irene S. Caldwell, *Responsible Adults in the Church School Program* (Anderson, Indiana: Warner Press, 1961), p. 14. Used by permission.

[5] Robert J. Havighurst, *Developmental Tasks and Education* (New York: Longmans, Green & Co., Inc.), p. 2.

[6] *Ibid.,* p. 72.

[7] Elton and Pauline Trueblood, *The Recovery of Family Life* (New York: Harper & Brothers, 1953), p. 45. Used by permission.

[8] Alphonse H. Clemens, *Marriage Education and Counseling* (Washington: Catholic University Press, 1951), p. 6.

[9] Edward K. Strong, Jr., *Change of Interests With Age* (New York: Oxford University Press).

[10] E. L. Thorndike, *Adult Interests* (New York: Macmillan Company).

[11] Caldwell, *op. cit.,* pp. 10, 11.

[12] Adapted from a chart in Elgin F. Hunt, *Social Science* (New York: Macmillan Company, 1955), p. 144.

CHAPTER 4

How to Understand Middle Adults

Defining Middle Adulthood

Middle adulthood is that period of life when adults reach their peak of achievement and should be happiest. Biologically it occurs at that transition between stability of growth and the beginning of growth decline. From a chronological point of view, the ages 36 to 55 will generally include the middle adult span. The ages of man could be charted as follows:

Acquisition from one to twelve.
Adjustment from thirteen to twenty-four.
Achievement from twenty-five to thirty-four.
Attainment from thirty-five to fifty.
Appraisal from fifty on.

According to this arrangement, the middle adult age is the age of attainment.

Dr. Earl F. Zeigler, widely known in adult Christian education circles, terms middle adulthood as "continuing adulthood."[1] He describes a typical middle-adult family in this manner:

The experiences through which this family have wended their way have made life a continuous adventure in sharing, worrying, adjusting and achieving. If reasonably successful, all can join in a glad *Te Deum.*[2]

Of course, all middle adults are not successful in making a life. Catastrophes and calamities, such as divorce, death, etc., often have marred the ideal. There are also adults whose lives must be touched by the gospel and who must pick up the frayed ends of disappointed life and attempt, with the help of Christ and His church, to redo what has been done.

Characteristics of Middle Adults

As has been indicated previously, some characteristics apply to all adults. One of these is their unlikeness. Spiritually, some adults are happy, well-adjusted, successful Christians; others are Christians living on the borderline. Some adults are cold, indifferent, and defeated with reference to the Christian faith. Psychologically, some are aggressive and self-confident while others are timid and hesitant. Some adults even have twisted personalities or are mentally deficient.

Other general characteristics include the ripening of physical and mental powers, greater ability to achieve, increased responsibility and growing stability, more persistent purposes, wider knowledge and richer experience. Perhaps on the debit side are such characteristics as set prejudices, fixed habits, overcautiousness, lack of vision, and inability to adjust easily. They will often dislike anything that is new or different. W. Edward Rafferty says, "We must not forget to reckon with a mental phenomenon which psychologists call 'neophobia'—fear of trying something new. Adults seem to be particularly susceptible to this malady. They can overcome it by realizing that civilization is always changing and that adaptation to the new is the law of growth." [3]

1. *Physical characteristics of middle adulthood.* Generally, middle adults enjoy good health, although this is the period when chronic ailments begin to develop. Of course, physical vigor is slightly depleted; movements are less active; heart action slows down; weight is added; and it becomes more difficult to throw off disease. The climacteric period of life is experienced and it may be characterized by physical pain, insomnia, sexual phantasies, or erratic and intensified sex desires. This physical reaction may have some moral implications if it is not properly channeled and controlled.

2. *Mental characteristics.* Middle adulthood is a time of productive mental power. Though there is a slight decrease in the rate of learning, more purposefulness, self-confidence, and a feeling of competence tend to offset this decrease, and wider knowledge is experienced by those who are mentally alert. This is the period of great achievement in mental tasks in spite of a developing cautiousness.

From a negative point of view, middle adults may become autocratic. Their vision may be restricted. Habits and prejudices may become so fixed as to cause them to be reactionary and unreasonable. In the latter part of this period mental stress and strain may produce harmful effects. This is a period when those who guide such adults need constantly to challenge them to greater mental endeavor and application so that Christian maturity may result.

3. *Social characteristics.* Socially, middle adults have reached the period of greatest achievement. Accepting increased burdens and responsibilities, they participate more in civic affairs. Since their children have all been raised or are well along in that process, more

time is available for social pursuits. This becomes the period of greatest service to others. Brewbaker, basing his conclusions upon Soares's *A Study of Adult Life,* says that the "period from forty to sixty is the most productive in human life . . . Vocationally, one has taken his place and is filling it with highest efficiency." He further states that "a study of adult leadership today would be a convincing proof of the vital place men and women in the middle life period hold in the world's progress and in human redemption." [4]

However, socially the middle adult is less adaptable. Adjustments to new situations are more difficult for him. Experience has often been a costly teacher. Disillusionment may come as faith in man's integrity and honesty comes into question through social interaction. However, as Andrews indicates, "If adults succeed in making their escape from 'the destruction that wasteth at noonday,' from the doubt and cynicism, that are apt to come at that period, the possibilities for soul expansion are incalculable." [5]

4. *Spiritual characteristics.* A person in middle adulthood will possess only those spiritual characteristics that have been nurtured into life in previous years. This should be a period of rich spiritual experience and extensive service to the program of the church. It will be if these adults have been properly guided in the past and are presently challenged by a vital program of enrichment provided by the church.

Too often, middle age becomes a time of moral laxity. The pressure of business and a tendency to take religious matters lightly combine to cause many to drift from the church. Consequently, commitment to immoral and unethical acts in business, social, and family relationships often follows. This need not be if adults are challenged to increase study of and devotion to the living Christ.

From a positive standpoint, it must be recognized that middle adults are the backbone of our congregations in numbers, leadership, and potential. Many are spiritually alert and willing to work in varying capacities to extend the kingdom. Though they may be more "set in their ways" than younger adults, they still are willing to learn and to adjust if properly challenged and motivated.

Needs and Problems of Middle Adults

The needs and problems of middle adults evolve out of the characteristics that have been mentioned. Such problems as personal health and happiness, family relationships, economic security, vocational satisfaction and prestige, the development of a circle of friends, and the advancement and nurture of their children are common to all adults. These problems must be frankly faced and solved if the adult is to be relatively satisfied with his life. The church can help in these various areas by providing instruction and a wholesome fellowship out of which adults may develop satisfactory solutions to these basic problems.

The church has the responsibility, through worship activities and guidance of learning, of meeting the basic spiritual needs of adults. Gaines S. Dobbins sees four basic needs of adults: (1) the need of a personal Saviour; (2) the need of sustaining motives; (3) the need of tested standards; and (4) the need of practical expression.[6] The adult Bible class, the Sunday-evening training program, and men's and women's groups can be utilized to win adults to Christ and His church, and help them reach Christian maturity. Through the evangelistic emphasis of the Bible school in its program of outreach and through the effort of adult teachers who teach for evangelistic results, adults can be led to acknowledging Christ as Saviour and committing their lives to Him in humble obedience. Continued instruction in the Sunday-morning Bible class and participation in an evening training program will help to sustain Christian motives and will be an aid to developing high moral standards by which everyday life may be lived with a view to honoring Christ through such a life. Through other activities and organizations of the church, middle adults can be enlisted in all sorts of practical activities, such as evangelistic calling, benevolent work, working with youth, participating in the stewardship program of the church, etc. The old adage, "Use them or lose them," is certainly applicable here.

Dr. Gorham approaches the needs of adults and ways in which the church may help satisfy these needs from a different standpoint.

1. *Adults need security*. The church may meet this need by providing comfort in time of trouble, counseling when problems arise, financial aid at crisis times, the answer to that crucial question, "Why are we here?"

2. *Middle adults need stimulation*. The church and its church school can help here through offering worship experiences by which the spirit is exalted, through group reinforcement of good intentions, through study of the Bible in which they are challenged and new understanding and enlarged horizons are gained.

3. *Middle adults need sociability*. Through fellowship activities in class and out they can find welcome within the Christian community. Compatible grouping in a well-designed adult graded program of study not only accomplishes much educationally, but also socially. The church school can also lead middle adults to

place greater emphasis upon family solidarity as it teaches the crucial nature of family life in the program of God.

4. *Middle adults need service.* Some means must be devised in each local congregation to discover the talent and ability of each adult. When this has been done, then these adults need to be challenged to individual and group service. No challenge, however, will be effective unless service activities are at hand in which to engage and unless practical guidance is given by which they may prosecute such activities competently.

The Church and Middle Adults

The church must consider the educational implications of middle adulthood. It must organize its program in such a way as to adequately challenge and to lead adults to a higher plane of Christian living. The adult characteristic of resisting change and the adult tendency to disregard, in many cases, the fact that the church is a spiritual democracy, should cause the church to exercise patience and understanding in perfecting the organization for adult education. Adults must be led to see that the Bible school is merely the church functioning in her educational task, not a separate agency unrelated to the total structure and pattern of church life.

Churches can meet the educational implications of middle adulthood by providing opportunities for effective study. Through the graded Sunday-morning Bible school adults should engage in an intense study of the Bible. This will involve smaller classes, better methods, greater application of each adult student, and a dependence upon God's spirit by both teacher and pupil. A Sunday-evening program of training in which adults will have opportunity to participate as well as learn needs to be launched in each local congregation. Studies in this program may include doctrine, church history, principles of effective churchmanship, leadership principles, and other such areas that would not normally be considered as direct Bible study. Beyond these two programs, special courses in leadership training, missions, stewardship, and evangelism might well be projected. Andrews reminds us that the characteristics, interests, needs, and problems of adults demand that the church realize that

the big end of the program of religious education for adults is to lead the adult to transfer the lessons of the sermon and the classroom to the market place and home. This is what Jesus meant when he told the cleansed Gadarene, "Go home to thy friends, and tell them how great things the Lord hath done for thee" (Mark 5:19). In telling it he would know it better. Nothing has such powerful moral reactions on oneself as practicing the lesson on others. [7]

The churches must also supply curriculum materials that are designed to meet the needs of middle adulthood. If the family and family relationships bulk large in middle adult life and constitute the greatest source of happiness for adults, then much curricular material should be aimed in this direction. Remember that curriculum grows out of our objectives and out of the needs of our students.

All in all, it is the responsibility of the church and its educational program to provide those activities of study, service, and fellowship that will challenge each adult to find his place in the ongoing advance of Christ's kingdom, and to successfully guide each middle adult through his years of greatest achievement.

Books for Further Study

ANDREWS, MATTHEW T. *Adults and the Art of Learning*. Nashville: Broadman Press, 1936.

DOBBINS, GAINES S. *Teaching Adults in the Sunday School*. Nashville: Sunday School Board.

GORHAM, DONALD R. *Understanding Adults*. Philadelphia: Judson Press, 1948.

POWELL, WILFRED E. *The Understanding of Adult Ways*. St. Louis: Bethany Press, 1914.

WESTPHAL, EDWARD P. *The Church's Opportunity in Adult Education*. Philadelphia: Westminster Press, 1941.

ZEIGLER, EARL F. *Christian Education of Adults*. Philadelphia: Westminster Press, 1958.

Questions for Discussion

1. What are the general age brackets into which middle adults can be classified?

2. Discuss the concept that middle adults are in their years of attainment.

3. Why do middle adults often develop a fear of trying something new?

4. What are some of the things the church can do to help middle adults successfully solve their spiritual problems?

5. Why is the principle, use them or lose them, especially applicable to this age group?

6. List some of the special interest areas of middle adults which could be developed through carefully chosen elective studies.

7. Make a study of your local church and observe what percentage of its leaders are middle adults.

8. Work out a program of Christian education for middle adults including suggested teaching materials, social functions, and service projects.

NOTES

[1] Earl F. Zeigler, *Christian Education of Adults* (Philadelphia: Westminster Press, 1958), p. 15.

[2] *Ibid.*

[3] W. Edmond Rafferty, *Religious Education of Adults* (New York: Fleming H. Revell Co., 1930), p. 60.

[4] Charles W. Brewbaker, *The Adult Program in the Church School* (New York: Fleming H. Revell Co., 1925), p. 24.

[5] Matthew T. Andrews, *Adults and the Art of Learning* (Nashville: Broadman Press, 1936), p. 49.

[6] Gaines S. Dobbins, *Teaching Adults in the Sunday School* (Nashville: Sunday School Board), pp. 54, 55.

[7] *Op. cit.*

CHAPTER 5

How to Understand Older Adults

It has only been in recent years that much attention has been given to the church's ministry to older adults. Why? Because only in this present century have we had so many older adults who need the church's ministry. Only as we know something of this twentieth-century phenomenon—the great increase of the aged and aging—can we understand the intense need of the church's concern.

Our Senior Citizens—A Growing Concern

Anyone who was born before 1900 in the United States could not reasonably expect to live beyond his forty-seventh birthday, since this was the statistical average of life expectancy at that time. Today the life span hovers around age 70. Great progress in public health and outstanding breakthroughs in preventive medicine have produced this outstanding fact.

There are now more than 15,000,000 people in the United States who are classified in the "aging" group. This represents 10 percent of the total population. Fifty-two percent of these are women. In the group above 70 years of age, the women outnumber the men almost two to one. Half of the aged women in the United States, and at least one-third of the men, are single or have lost their helpmates through death or divorce. Some 5,000,000 of our older adults are still working. From one-tenth to one-third of all older citizens are chronically ill despite the great advances in medical science.

Characteristics of Older Adults

There are certain characteristics and needs that tend to cluster around the "aging" just as was noted in the previous chapters on young adulthood and middle adulthood. These are a combination of physical, emotional, social, and spiritual factors as they affect those in the latter stage of earthly existence.

1. *Physical.* Physically such things as partial loss of vision and hearing, loss of appetite, chronic illness, and nervous irritability characterize this age group.

2. *Emotional.* Emotionally, frustration, anxiety, and anger may be present due to improper adjustment to problems that are faced.

3. *Social.* Socially, isolationism may result due to an unwillingness to participate actively in creative living. These are not only characteristics that may be seen, they are problems to be faced not only by the person himself but by those who are close to him (such as relatives) and those who would attempt to help him make a senior citizenship a time of fullness and satisfaction.

4. *Withdrawal.* Such "danger signals" as "apathy, listlessness, disinterest, boredom, seclusiveness, repeated complaints of poor health, 'crying jags,' and unwarranted outbursts of anger"[1] indicate that the person is approaching that stage called "old age."

5. *A sense of loss.* Perhaps a dominating characteristic of older people is that attitude produced by a sense of loss—loss of things they once had or the threat of loss of things they still possess. Great Aunt Sue complains constantly because she has lost her sense of usefulness. Grandpa Jones threatens, blusters, and shouts angrily at everything and everyone to cover up his loss of power when his income is cut by retirement. These losses include both tangible and intangible things. Loss of income, family, and health are most obvious. Such losses as that of prestige and status, identity, and even self-respect are psychological and subjective, but they must be seen as realities that often trigger irrational and unrelated behavioral patterns. The loss of love, whether real or imagined, is particularly threatening. The oldster reasons that he is not loved since he is no longer useful. This may lead to isolationism and withdrawal and to a general apathy. We must seek ways and means of showing these senior citizens that they are loved and respected. We must help them see that their losses can be compensated for in other ways.

Needs of Older Adults

The need for "growing," for making adjustments, confronts every age. Though we use the concept "developmental tasks" primarily with younger people, yet there is a sense in which our senior citizens also face "developmental tasks." There are tasks or adjustments that they must accomplish in order that they may not live out their closing days in regret. Dr. Earl Zeigler lists these "adjustments" or "tasks" which older adults need to make:[2]

1. Adjusting to retirement and generally reduced income.
2. Adjusting to bodily changes, disabilities, and gerontological diseases.
3. Adjusting to loss of mate, old friends, and relatives.
4. Adjusting to different housing arrangements.
5. Adjusting to one's own age group and to younger age groups.

6. Adjusting to the changing requirements of a complex civilization.
7. Adjusting to a different role in leadership, vocation, and other responsibilities.
8. Adjusting to the inevitable fact of death.
9. Adjusting to the acceptance of continuing contribution to citizenship responsibilities in community, national, and international affairs.
10. Adjusting to social responsibilities.
11. Adjusting to living with oneself.

At both a National Conference on the Aging held in Washington, D.C., and at an International Conference on the Church and Older Persons held at Lake Geneva, Wisconsin, older people, who were delegates to these conferences, helped prepare a list of basic spiritual needs. This list included such items as the following:

1. Assurance of God's continuing love.
2. The certainty that life is protected.
3. Relief from heightened emotions (especially guilt, grief, fear).
4. Relief from pangs of loneliness.
5. A perspective (for life) that embraces time and eternity.
6. Continuing spiritual growth through new experiences.
7. Satisfying status in life as a person.
8. A feeling of continuing usefulness.[3]

If these spiritual needs are met, the sense of loss which is so prevalent among adults will be overcome to a large degree. "The losses are, for the most part, in the realm of the physical and the sensuous. The compensations are, broadly speaking, in the realm of the personal and the spiritual. This makes the Christian faith peculiarly relevant to the adjustments demanded by later maturity."[4]

The Church's Responsibility to Older Adults

Maves and Cedarleaf maintain that "in view of the rising tide of interest in older people . . . a careful study of religious ministry to older people is imperative." They add, significantly:

The minister and the church cannot sidestep the problems of an aging population without considerable loss of effectiveness and relevance in our present situation. Neither can they minister to the younger generations effectively while neglecting the older people, for they form a very important part of the human climate in which youth is nurtured.[5]

The church that would minister effectively to older adults must develop certain basic principles or objectives that will guide the projected program or programs initiated for senior citizens within the church. These objectives or principles will vary with each congregation since every congregation has specific needs, but the following suggestions are general and flexible enough to be utilized by every congregation concerned with older adult work.

1. *Assess the needs of your church and community.* Is the proportion of older people large or small? What is being done for older people spiritually? Are their spiritual needs (see page 37) being met by current church programs?

2. *Cooperate as far as possible with community or civic programs for the aging.* (e. g., If the community provides a golden age club where new interests may be developed, work through this community provision rather than in competition with it.)

3. *Provide leadership.* Leadership is essential, but this leadership must be accepted. Perhaps for older people a contemporary—one who "has been there"—will be most suitable as a leader. Elsie T. Culver says that

The older person who by temperament, natural endowments, education, and experience, stands but as a leader in the older group within the church, has thereby a great responsibility—not so much to do things *for* his contemporaries (he must protect himself from that!), but to help them to understand and do things for themselves.[6]

Some larger churches may wish to find such a qualified leader to add to the staff for a special ministry to older adults.

4. *Let older people help plan their own programs.* It will be theirs, then, and not something forced upon them. They will feel a responsibility in seeing that the program is executed. This will also provide continued opportunities of service and usefulness to those involved in the planning.

5. *Use group-work principles.* The group-workshop principle is in keeping with the Biblical concept of "fellowship." Encourage democratic procedures, centering the program around persons who have been enlisted in group responsibility. Let all activities flow from the group as expressions of their partnership together.

6. *Remember that older people need fun too.* Recreational and social activities for these who have much leisure time should be provided. If this is done adequately through civic effort, the local church needs to encourage the aging to utilize these provisions. If not, the congregation can itself provide a "senior center" where games, hobbies, interests, etc., can be developed and encouraged.

7. *Do not overlook the individual person.* Many older adults will be unable to participate in the regular programs provided for their age group. Personal counsel and encouragement through regular visitation need to be provided in such cases.

The Church's Program for Older Adults

In light of these objectives, the various organizations of the church must plan for meeting older adult needs. The regular church-school program should be so graded as to provide classes for older adults where worship, fellowship, and study will continue to mold these persons into more mature Christian patterns. Learning continues throughout life and many older adults will still have an insatiable thirst for Biblical and spiritual knowledge. Many of these older adults may be used as teachers in the church school, for they often have more time for study, research, and experimentation with new methods that younger teachers will not have.

The Extension Department of the church school will have a vital part to play in providing for later adults. Many of these will be invalid, unable to attend the regular church gatherings and functions. A real ministry can be carried out by bringing the benefits of study and worship to these shut-ins. Visitation with these older members of the church may be guided by these principles:

1. *Have regular times for visiting these older shut-ins.* The anticipation of your visit will be pleasurable to the older person.

2. *Have a definite idea as to what you will want to talk about during your visit.* Don't just chitchat.

3. *Bring some "paper," article, or other object along to serve as a "conversation piece."* Presents or surprises are always welcome and need not be expensive. Letters, books or magazines (from the church library), plants, greeting cards (perhaps made by one of the children's classes or groups), etc., could be used in this way.

4. *Allow reasonable time for a constructive visit.*

5. *Listen carefully when the older person is talking.* You will get new clues to their interests, hopes, fears, and feelings. Do not, however, be overly sympathetic when they chronically complain. Change the subject.

6. *Do not argue with nor criticize these older people.* Keep the conversation positive.

7. *Let the older people do as much for you and themselves as they are willing and able.* Don't jump up to do things that they would wish to do as hosts or hostesses in their homes. Accept their gifts graciously though you may not like or need them. Remember, they want to feel useful and it gives them a sense of satisfaction to give you a gift or do some favor for you.

8. *Above all, be yourself with these older people.* They will appreciate your sincerity, and a relationship of trust and friendship will develop that will be mutually beneficial.

9. *Leave with a word of encouragement, a Scripture thought,*

a prayer, or some other spiritual emphasis. Remember, you are Christ's minister, a priest of God, helping someone else to find a closer fellowship and relationship with Him.

Golden Age Clubs

Golden Age Clubs, or Senior centers, designed for recreation, social life, study, fellowship—in short, the use of leisure time profitably—may be developed if the need is sufficient. These may meet in strategic locations in the community or in the church building (many larger churches plan for such a center in their new buildings just as they plan for a nursery).

Other activities in which older adults may be enlisted are visitation (if qualified and health permits), drama, benevolence, worship, and service projects. Having more leisure time, they are often an untapped source of larger service for many church programs and activities.

Conclusion

The preacher of Ecclesiastes urges that his hearers remember their Creator in the days of their youth "while the evil days come not, nor the years draw nigh, when thou shalt say, I have no pleasure in them" (Ecclesiastes 12:1). In this passage he points out a truth that has relevance for our study—later maturity needs preparation. If the church, through its program of teaching, training, worship, fellowship, and service, has built into persons correct spiritual attitudes and willing dedication, then the transition to older adulthood will be made graciously and the older adult will look forward to the future creatively and hopefully.

Books for Further Study

CEDARLEAF, J. LENNART, and MAVES, PAUL B. *Older People and the Church.* New York: Abingdon Press, 1959. Excellent.

CULVER, ELSIE T. *New Church Programs With the Aging.* New York: Association Press, 1961. (See this for an excellent bibliography.)

HOWE, REUEL L. *The Creative Years.* Greenwich, Conn.: Seabury Press, Inc., 1958.

LAWTON, GEORGE. *Aging Successfully.* New York: Columbia University Press, 1946.

MOON, ALLEEN. *The Christian Education of Older People.* Nashville: Cokesbury Press, 1943.

NARRAMORE, CLYDE M. *The Mature Years.* Grand Rapids: Zondervan Publishing House, 1961.

SCHIFFERES, JUSTUS J. *The Older People in Your Life.* New York: Pocket Books, Inc., 1962.

STAFFORD, VIRGINIA, and EISENBERG, LARRY. *Fun for Older Adults*. New York: Abingdon Press, 1956.

Questions for Discussion

1. What are some of the current factors that should cause the church to take special note of the aging?

2. In a brief sentence describe each of the following characteristics of older adults: physical, emotional, and social.

3. List ten adjustments older adults usually have to make.

4. Select three adjustments from the list above and show how the church can give valuable assistance to its older adults in making them.

5. Why is a spiritual emphasis in an adult curriculum extremely important?

6. What specific adult elective studies would you suggest to meet the spiritual needs listed in the report by the National Conference on the Aging?

7. Why is it important to let older people share in the planning of their class and social activities?

8. Outline the program now being used by the Extension Department of your church school. If one is not in operation, draw up a complete program that you feel would be effective in view of the information in this chapter.

9. Describe in your own words an effective visit to a shut-in.

10. What is a Golden Age Club?

NOTES

[1] Justus J. Schifferes, *The Older People in Your Life* (New York: Pocket Books, Inc., 1962), p. 13.

[2] Earl F. Zeigler, *Christian Education of Adults* (Philadelphia: Westminster Press, © 1958, W. L. Jenkins), pp. 121, 122. Used by permission.

[3] *Ibid.*, p. 121.

[4] Paul B. Maves and J. Lennart Cedarleaf, *Older People and the Church* (New York: Abingdon Press, 1959), p. 71.

[5] *Ibid.*, p. 22.

[6] Elsie T. Culver, *New Church Programs With the Aging* (New York: Association Press, 1961), p. 56.

CHAPTER 6

How Adults Learn

It is difficult to answer the question, What is learning? In one sense there is no answer to this question just as there is no answer to other questions about dynamic entities in our experience, such as electricity, time, and love. We may be able to induct and use electricity, but we cannot define it adequately. Time is taken for granted as essential to life, but how difficult it is to accurately define it. We understand and are engulfed in love, and see demonstrations of it day by day, but who can express its dynamic nature in words? So it is with learning. We can observe its course and character, its process; but it is impossible to pin it down with a neatly-packaged definition. It is far more important that we know how to cause it to take place than it is to define it.

Learning is a term used to cover a variety of activities. Learning is applied to such experiences as memorizing Scripture, acquiring the skill to drive a car or ride a bicycle, developing attitudes and prejudices, and developing the ability to reason abstractly. These activities are not all alike, yet we apply the term learning to each. It is quite easily seen that a definition of learning would vary depending upon the activity or experience referred to by the term. Kenneth Benne looks at learning from the basis of this variation in learning experience:

Learning may be thought of as acquisition and mastery by a person of what is already known on some subject.

Learning may also be thought of as the extension and clarification of meanings of one's own individual experience.

Learning is a process (in which) one tests ideas and generalizations relevant to some delimitable problems, and tests them in some more or less objectified and controlled experiences designed for the purpose.[1]

Although it is difficult to define learning adequately or accurately, this generalized definition is suggested: *Learning takes place when desirable changes have resulted in human behavior.* Though this will not satisfy the educational theorist, it will give us some base of operation from which we may attack the problem of learning. After considering some of the areas where changes must take place, we shall consider some of the current theories of the learning process.

Areas of Learning

As has been indicated, learning refers to various kinds of human experience and activity. A psychologist, Tolman, has suggested that there are at least seven kinds of learning. Perhaps these areas or kinds of learning could be subsumed in four general classifications—knowledge, skill, attitude, and appreciation. When desirable changes have taken place in these areas, learning has been achieved.

1. *Knowledge*. Knowledge has to do with being acquainted with facts, events, and principles and understanding their meaning and relationship. Other words somewhat synonymous with knowledge are wisdom and information. Wisdom is the capacity of judging soundly and dealing broadly with facts learned, especially in their relation to practical life and conduct. Wisdom often "implies depth of insight or ripeness of experience" (Webster). We would desire in our teacher-learner experience that students not only gain knowledge but also develop wisdom. This is particularly stressed in the book of Proverbs and the epistles of Paul. Information is "knowledge communicated or acquired especially by reading or observation" (Webster).

If knowledge is a significant achievement in learning, then it follows that there must be a certain amount of transmission involved in teaching. In its technical sense, there is nothing wrong with indoctrination, for it means the impartation of knowledge or facts. This is particularly important in Christian education, for there is a content—the gospel and its historical setting—which must be known and understood before desirable changes in human behavior are possible.

2. *Skill*. J. L. Corzine defines skill as "the ability to do some act with ease and accuracy." It is a "developed or acquired ability," "a technical proficiency," according to Webster. Much of our learning is within this area. From infancy we develop skills by observing parents and playmates, by personal trial-and-error methods, and by constant practice. Cooking, driving, athletic proficiency, etc., all fall into this category. But there are skills to be learned in connection with local church work and activity. Soul winning, public prayer, directing worship, and teaching Bible-school classes all demand skill or technical proficiency.

3. *Attitudes*. An attitude is a habitual way of thinking and feeling about persons, relations, and things. Attitudes and sentiments are somewhat synonymous. These are learned; they are not inherent, nor do they just happen. Since negative attitudes are often prejudicial, this area of learning will involve some negativism. Some

attempts must be made to destroy wrong attitudes in order to make way for right attitudes. Jesus had much to say about attitudes and their importance to life. The attitude of hate leads to murder (Matthew 5:21-25). Personal lust leads to adultery (Matthew 5:27-32). One's attitude toward wealth and things may save or damn him for eternity (Matthew 6:19, 20; 25-34; Luke 12:16-21; 18:18-30). The attitude of love toward God and man constitutes the very basis of the moral life (Matthew 22:34-40).

4. *Appreciation.* Corzine says that appreciation is "the ability to assign values." This is certainly a valid category of learning experience, especially within Christian education. Values are important to life, and the ability to make proper assessment of what is most significantly valuable is imperative. "Ye cannot serve God and mammon," said Jesus, and He calls upon His followers to assess the relative value of these "two masters" and forsake mammon for God. We must, then, learn appreciation in order that we may be disciples of Jesus and be able to give ourselves to the higher values of life.

These categories are not watertight compartments. They merge and blend into one another. One learns attitudes and appreciation only as prior knowledge makes it possible. Skill and knowledge are also inseparable. One must know before he can do! Life is a totality with various areas of experience distinguishable within this totality; learning must also be seen in this same way.

Theories of Learning

The process of learning is built upon an understanding of man —his nature, behavior, and motivation. Just as there have been many theories put forth to understand human behavior (schools of psychology), so there have been many theories propounded concerning an understanding of the process of human learning. Both— theories of behavior and theories of learning—are based solidly upon the assumptions held in regard to the nature of man.

Let us illustrate: Philosophers who emphasized the rationality of man, emphasized the molding influence of rationality in both human behavior and learning. To the question, "Why do people behave as they do?" they would answer, "When they understand what they are to do they will do it." Learning then became solely a matter of providing knowledge. Other philosophers, emphasizing the cruciality of the pleasure principle, would answer the same question with "They are getting pleasure out of it. That's why they do it." Learning then would be accomplished by contriving pleasurable experiences leading to worthwhile goals. Other philosophers, seeing instincts or sex drives as central, would naturally develop learning theories that are compatible with their basic philosophy.

The Christian approaches the nature of man from a Biblical perspective. It follows that a Christian's theory of learning must be in harmony with Biblical data. Man as a creature of God, yet created in God's image; man as sinner, yet responsible for his plight; man as rational, yet often overwhelmed by rampaging emotions; man as individual, yet as an integral part of society and molded by group experience—all these are emphases to be found in Scripture. Our learning theory, then, must be developed in light of these basic facts.

1. *Trial and error.* Surprisingly, though many theories of learning cannot be accepted *en toto,* there are many insights in all the various theories that are compatible with both Biblical and scientific facts. E. L. Thorndike's *connectionism* with its emphasis upon trial and error and stimulus-response bonds, though defective when seen as the total explanation of learning, gives us some insight into how we learn. The laws of readiness, effect, and exercise that he framed stimulate several suggestions. His emphasis upon the readiness of the organism (individual) for learning experience helps us to understand how important our approach to a class session and our pupils really is. The old adage, "Use it or lose it," Thorndike shows, has bearing upon learning. Repetition and practice are imperative. His stress on the pleasure-pain concept in learning (we learn only when learning is accompanied by pleasure), though only partially true, is an acceptable principle, by and large.

But Thorndike's theory is unacceptable as a theory to account for the totality of learning processes. There are too many problems left unexplained. His theory structure rested too much on animal rather than human experimentation. The higher, more abstract areas of learning were not dealt with adequately.

2. *Environmental conditioning.* Learning as *conditioning* was later developed by Pavlov and J. B. Watson. Pavlov's experiments in Russia with the conditioning of animals were interpreted so as to make the conditioned reflex the significant unit in learning. J. B. Watson, who was totally mechanistic in his approach to human behavior, became the promoter of the *conditioned reflex* or *conditioned response* as the total explanation of how we learn. Here again there is an element of truth. Some learning is achieved through conditioning. We can fix certain desirable habits or break undesirable habits through conditioning. The environmental conditioning of learning is important. This is why we attempt to make

the place of learning (classroom, church building) a pleasant, agreeable, satisfying place. This is why it is important for the student not to be humiliated or made to feel inferior or out of place while learning. Such conditions will often deter the learning process.

Again, though acceptable in part, conditioning cannot make room for all the facts. How does one account for that learning that takes place in spite of improper conditioning? Other higher factors as purpose, goal, and needs seem to enter in. Abstract learning is also inexplicable in the light of mechanistic and behavioristic conditioning.

3. *Gestalt—consideration of the whole*. The strongest criticism leveled at both Thorndike and the exponents of conditioning was that these theorists were too concerned about small units or particles or pieces of learning. Those critics who felt that emphasis should be placed upon the *whole* rather than its parts, upon patterns rather than upon single incidents of learning, have been called *gestalt* (a German word meaning shape, form, pattern, configuration) psychologists. Their experiments tended to show that learning does not result from random activity (trial and error) or mechanistic conditioning, but through perceiving relationships and gaining insights. Purposes and goals also were seen as significant factors in the learning process.

Others, as Edward C. Tolman, have taken this concept of goal or purpose and made it the most significant factor in learning. Kidd analyzes this emphasis in the following manner:

> Tolman insists that behavior is directed in relation to goals. It is always moving toward something or away from something. What is significant about what an animal or a man is doing is *what he is doing it for*. The learner selects the means or tools for achieving his purpose and he chooses what he will learn in relation to some purpose; learning doesn't happen by chance. For him there is also a principle of least effort: the learner tends to select the means which will most easily and most quickly achieve his purpose. Because this is so, Tolman believes, people are teachable; they make good learners.[2]

From a Biblical standpoint this approach is much more acceptable than that of Thorndike or Watson. Man is seen as a responsible person who has goals and who chooses what he learns and how he learns in relation to these goals. We reject any theory of learning that questions man's possession of a subjective will.

4. *Group dynamics*. The most recent theories relating to learning center around group dynamics. This theory is primarily the results of the influence of social psychology and sociology upon

education. Whether these theories will supplant the earlier theories, time alone will tell; at least they suggest a depth to the total structure of learning that must not be overlooked. Generally, we learn in groups; our role in the group and the self-picture that we develop in connection with this role has an important bearing upon learning.

5. *Psychoanalysis.* Other approaches, such as *psychoanalysis*, have given some insight into certain aspects of learning and human behavior. The importance of unconscious influences, the bearing of fixation (an arrested development in which an adult may continue at an adolescent level of behavior), repression (attempting to ignore or avoid unhappy experiences by relegating them to the subconscious), regression (returning to earlier modes of behavior) upon learning, and the way in which fear and anxiety inhibit or promote learning have all been contributed from the psychoanalytical field developed by Sigmund Freud.

As we stated in the beginning of this discussion, we cannot accept any of these theories *en toto.* However, by way of summary there are certain values to be derived from a knowledge of them. The following points are worthy of careful consideration. (1) From *connectionism* we are reminded of the importance of using the proper approach to the lesson and the pupil in the teaching process. (2) From *environmental conditioning* we are made aware of the importance of a pleasant, agreeable classroom in the learning process. (3) From *gestalt* we are pointed to the importance of establishing broad goals for our teaching. (4) From *group dynamics* we are reminded to always teach with the group situation in mind. (5) And finally, from *psychoanalysis* we can become aware of some of the mental attitudes that stimulate and retard the learning process.

Factors Involved in Learning

There are a number of factors involved in the learning process. To understand in some measure these factors will give us greater insight into the course of learning.

1. *Need.* The need to receive appreciation and affection, to experience love, is certainly universal. The need to share in some cooperative endeavor, to have some opportunity of participating in or making some contribution to worthwhile endeavors, is to be found everywhere. The need to grow, to meet new experiences, and to attain some measure of understanding and insight also seems to be universal. C. M. Fleming charts these needs in relation to associated forms of expression and experience in this manner:

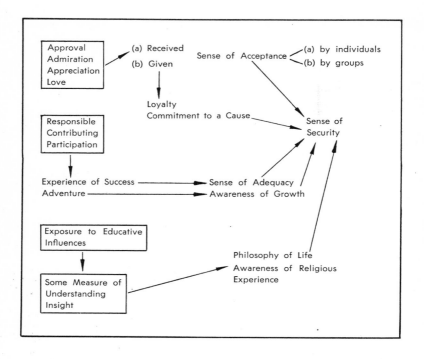

The educative process must be closely related to and allied with these needs.

2. *Self.* One's concept of self will determine ease of learning, for a confident self will approach the task of learning optimistically and the success achieved in learning will bolster confidence and strengthen one's picture of himself. Often a teacher is faced with a student whose self-concept is so self-abasing that the student has no confidence in his ability to learn. When the teacher helps orient this student toward a better concept of self, then the student will become more confident and will be able to achieve success in the experience of learning.

3. *Relationship.* Learning takes place in relationship. Though some learning is isolated, most learning is done in relationship to others. It is important that this relationship (whether between teacher and learner or learner and learner) be one of mutual respect, love, and trust. Only as we trust individuals as human personalities to be respected and loved will effective learning result.

4. *Purposive, thought-producing activity.* We learn by doing! This does not mean, however, that random activity is educational.

Actually we learn by *thinking* about what we are doing! This is especially true of the learning situation where we are teaching moral, spiritual, or idealistic concepts.

5. *Meaningfulness.* Learning can take place only where motivation, practice, and reinforcement are present. Psychological tests have shown that even simple things are easier learned when meaning is apparent. Stephens says that "there is no question that meaningful, highly structured material is easier to grasp, easier to learn and easier to remember." [3]

Meaningfulness leads to insight, and insight is the result of learning; in fact, some educational psychologists (following the *gestalt* lead) believe that insight is the central point of learning.

6. *Problem-solving.* At one time, the concept of problem-solving was suggested as being basic to the educational process. John Dewey, in *How We Think,* popularized this concept. He felt that thinking (and, consequently, learning) followed this pattern:

a. Diagnose the problem.

b. Cast about for solutions to the problem.

c. Suggest possible solutions.

d. Test these solutions out.

It is readily seen that we often learn in this manner. This is why projects, challenging assignments, etc., have great value in assisting the pupil to learn.

Summary

Apparently, as one surveys all the varied factors that are a part of the learning process, it is quite complex. Any theory of learning that over-simplifies must be rejected. Learning is active, not passive, and the learner brings to the task all past images, experiences, memories, emotions, and his needs. Out of these a new structure or organization is created as new ideas, skills, or attitudes are assimilated. But the individual does not learn in isolation nor in an individualistic manner; he learns within a social climate and brings to learning certain social attitudes as to his self and his role in relation to the group life of which he is a part.

Irene S. Caldwell, relating learning to adults and stating it quite simply, says: "Adults learn best when they have a sense of need, resulting in a desire to learn; when they have a feeling of being personally involved in the issue at hand; when they put forth real effort to put new ideas into practice; and when a feeling of satisfaction results from the learning experience." [4] This points up the need for the teacher to always apply the lesson facts and use some method of evaluating the pupil's response.

The Teacher's Responsibility in Learning

The teacher of adults (as well as any age group) must recognize that learning is an active process. The pupil must do the learning! All the teacher can do is provide materials, methods, motivation, and interest and create an atmosphere that makes learning possible and desirable on the part of the student. Thus, the teacher needs to know something about learning theories, effective methods to be used with the age group in question, and something of the personality development of that age group. Above all, the teacher needs to have clearly in mind the objectives of Christian teaching. He must ask, "What changes do we want to occur? What kind of persons do we want our pupils to become? What do we want them to know, to do, to feel, to think?" Unless the teacher can answer these questions satisfactorily in light of Biblical truth, learning will not likely take place.

Books for Further Study

CALDWELL, IRENE S. *Adults Learn and Like It.* Anderson, Indiana: Warner Press, 1955.

CORZINE, J. L. *Looking at Learning.* Nashville: Convention Press, 1957.

FLEMING, CHARLOTTE M. *Teaching, a Psychological Analysis.* New York: John Wiley & Sons, Inc.

HILGARD, ERNEST R. *Theories of Learning.* New York: Appleton-Century-Crofts, Inc., 1948.

KIDD, J. R. *How Adults Learn.* New York: Association Press, 1959.

STEPHENS, JOHN M. *Educational Psychology.* New York: Holt, Rinehart and Winston, Inc.

THORNDIKE, E. L. *The Fundamentals of Learning.* New York: Teacher's College, Columbia University, 1932.

Questions for Discussion

1. Why is it difficult to define learning? What definition has been used in this chapter?

2. Name the four areas of life that a teacher should observe in a pupil whether or not learning has taken place.

3. What three things about the nature of man needs to be understood when making a study of the process of learning?

4. What bearing does one's philosophy about the nature of man have on his theory of learning?

5. Name five theories of learning.

6. Explain Thorndike's theory of correctionism.

7. Why doesn't the environmental conditioning theory fully explain the learning process?

8. Name five factors that are involved in the learning process.

9. What was the pattern for learning that John Dewey suggested?

10. What are some of the objectives a teacher needs to decide before setting up a teaching situation?

NOTES

[1] Carl R. Rogers, *Counseling and Psychotherapy* (Boston: Houghton Mifflin Company, 1948).

[2] J. R. Kidd, *How Adults Learn* (New York: Association Press, 1959), p. 163. Used by permission.

[3] John M. Stephens, *Educational Psychology* (New York: Holt, Rinehart and Winston, Inc.), p. 353.

[4] Irene S. Caldwell, *Adults Learn and Like It* (Anderson, Indiana: Warner Press, 1955), pp. 18, 19. Used by permission.

CHAPTER 7

Teaching Methods for Adults

Prior to the twentieth century only two methods of Christian education were generally used. One was the lecture method where the teacher was considered to be in complete command of the material and the class. The other was the question-and-answer method. The latter was almost always employed in the teaching of catechism. Since at this time children were considered to be merely "miniature adults," the same methods were employed in teaching them.

The dawn of the twentieth century brought new developments in all fields of education. Psychology brought a new understanding of human nature. New studies were made of motivations for learning that were helpful. The results were a whole series of new techniques for teaching.

Characteristics of the Newer Methods

1. *They are true to life.* They relate materials, facts, and meanings to real-life situations. Knowledge is seen as a tool, not a mere end in itself. We learn in order to be more effective persons.

2. *There is more responsibility on the pupil.* Newer methods attempt to involve the individual learner in the learning process; therefore it assumes that the student will be an active participant in the learning process, not merely a passive recipient.

3. *They treat the pupil as a person.* The newer methods recognize that each student is a person with basic needs—physical, emotional, mental, and spiritual. They seek to motivate learning through an understanding of the student as a person.

4. *They give a new emphasis to social concepts.* Recent studies of human life have shown that men are social beings, and that their behavior is determined by the group relations that they sustain. Group dynamics and principles of group leadership are considered significant in modern educational methodology. What one's status or role is within the group—whether a Bible-school class, a youth fellowship group, or a church board—often is indicative of how well that person will learn. The relation between student and teacher is also important within the newer concepts of methods.

5. *They are based upon a study of personality development.* The newer methods recognize that persons develop, and that one can know something of a person's interests, attitudes, and capabilities at any stage of development. They emphasize that teaching techniques will be related to this basic understanding of human development.

Factors That Determine Your Methods

1. *The aim of the class session.* No method will be used, of course, that is out of harmony with the ultimate purpose of relating people to God through Jesus Christ. More specifically, the aim of a particular lesson will to some degree indicate the approach the teacher will use. If you desire to increase Biblical knowledge, those methods that attempt to present facts in a systematic manner should be used. If the desire is to develop some skill, then some type of drill method may be used. In other words, the method must be correlated with the purpose of teaching.

2. *The maturity of the pupils.* Educational leaders, through an understanding of the development of individuals, have found that certain methods are more effective with certain age groups. It would be foolish to expect three-year-old children to enter into an informal group discussion, for they do not have the capacity to participate in such a learning experience. Likewise, it would be humiliating for a teacher to treat adults as children and constantly use a method best suited for children, such as the story method.

3. *The attitude of the students toward learning.* If the class is eager, the teacher may choose such methods as project, discussion, etc., which demand cooperation and active participation. On the other hand, if there is a lackadaisical or indifferent attitude such methods would be ineffective. A competent teacher must be sensitive to his pupils' attitudes and attempt to gauge his use of methods accordingly.

4. *The class's background and previous study.* A class of new converts whose background in Biblical knowledge is meager must be approached in a different way than a class made up of mature Christians. The lecture method is justifiable in presenting relatively new material to students who have had no previous study in this field. On the other hand, students who have a good Biblical foundation may be unchallenged by the lecture method if it involves only the presentation of familiar facts. Students, no matter what their age may be, do not learn unless their intellectual powers are challenged in some vital way.

5. *The nature of the material used in teaching.* The materials provided for a given class session may give us a clue as to what method could best be used to bring about maximum learning. If we are to deal with an incident in the life of a well-known Biblical character, perhaps the lecture-story method would be our best approach. If we are to study the Christian's attitude toward a personal or social problem, discussion may prove most beneficial. The content of the material must be studied carefully before a method is selected.

6. *Physical equipment and facilities.* Teachers are often limited by space and lack of proper facilities. Such methods as research and the project require certain facilities which may or may not be available. Questions such as these need to be asked: Is there a library provided? Are there chalkboards or maps? Are visual aids provided? If these questions are answered negatively, then methods using these facilities or items of equipment cannot be used. Of course, all the facilities that can possibly be provided ought to be made available so that Christian teaching can be effective.

7. *The amount of time the teacher has.* The Bible school that provides only thirty minutes of actual teaching time cannot expect its teachers to use some very good methods. It may be that teachers rely upon the lecture method because they do not have adequate time to use other methods effectively. Such methods as discussion and the project are time-consuming by their very nature, and most teachers, even if they were competent to use these methods, would not have the time to do so in many church schools.

8. *The skill and qualifications of the individual teacher.* A teacher cannot use any method effectively if he has no ability in the use of such a method. It is impractical to expect teachers to use methods in which they have not been trained. Hence, it is important that each local congregation provide a leadership training program to introduce prospective teachers to the various methods of Christian teaching and provide opportunities for developing skill in the use of these methods.

All of these factors are important. The adult teacher will carefully assess his own situation, considering these various factors, and then choose a method that will provide the best opportunity for his adult students to learn. He must remember, however, that all methods have strengths and weaknesses. No one method is *best* for every situation and no one method is *best* for every teacher. Each teacher should analyze his own approach, continue to use those methods in which he has some skill, and attempt to develop skill in other methods.

Types of Methods

The Lecture Method

The lecture method is not only one of the oldest methods known to men, but it is also the most frequently used in the Bible school today. With adults, its use is almost standard. Only a few creative teachers are willing to break with tradition and use other methods. Though there has been much criticism of this method, it should be recognized that such criticism should be leveled not at the method itself but at the abuses of it.

Some advantages of the lecture method are listed below:

1. It conserves time.

2. It provides a basis of authority if the lecturer is an expert in his field.

3. It is a method in which the teacher has complete control of the teaching situation.

4. It is a method that can be combined with other methods (such as discussion and question-and-answer) in an effective manner.

5. It is popular with most adults.

6. It provides an opportunity for the lecturer to influence, by means of his personality, those who listen.

The following are disadvantages of the lecture method:

1. There is a minimum of student participation.

2. The lecture method often does not take into consideration individual differences.

3. The lecturer may not be effective in controlling the students in his class.

4. The teacher seldom knows whether or not he is stimulating interest and keeping attention.

5. The lecture may become a drab, rather monotonous experience.

6. The lecture method may be used to cover up a teacher's inadequacy or ignorance.

Here are seven steps for lecture improvement:

Step one: "Your attention, please"	Focus the attention of the class on the business at hand by using a story, a question, a picture, or a performance.
Step two: "Here goes"	Tell your class what the lesson is going to be about and why it is important to them. Present the key facts in logical sequence.

55

Step three: "For example"	Tie the lesson down with examples from experience, history, or current events, or with a brief quotation. Do not hold all the application to the end of the lecture; weave it throughout the lesson.
Step four: "Got it?"	Insert pertinent questions either to be answered audibly or mentally. Help your pupils check up on their learning by asking, "Why, Joe"; "How, Mary"; "What, Bill," etc.
Step five: "The Bible says"	Make sure the important points of your lecture are based on Bible truths. Show how the Bible solves life's problems and meets everyday needs.
Step six: "In conclusion"	Summarize the crux of your lesson material and lesson application with a concise restatement of your main points.
Step seven: "Do this"	Assign some specific task for home study or practical service that grows out of the lesson or will serve to introduce the lesson for the coming week.

The Discussion Method

In recent years, the discussion method has become a most popular method of education. Most adults like to talk, and, if given an opportunity and the proper challenge, they can be led to participate in an excellent discussion. Of course, there is more to the discussion method than simply talking. Findley B. Edge defines the discussion as "a cooperative search for truth in seeking the solution to a problem." [1] The teacher should attempt to involve all members of the class or group to participate. The value of this method is not only to arrive at truth through a cooperative effort, but to effect changes in the lives and thinking of the participants.

The key to a successful discussion is the teacher or leader.

The following are responsibilities of the leader:

1. The leader should be careful not to dominate the discussion by answering every question or constantly expressing his own views in a dominant manner.

2. The leader should be well informed on the question or problem being discussed. New approaches, issues, and problems should be introduced by him.

3. Keep an air of informality by inserting humor, asking class members to remain seated as they speak, using first names, and having the arrangements of chairs, etc., conducive to informality.

4. Be sure that all members understand the question. Write it on the chalkboard. Give an introductory statement indicating why

the question or problem is important or how it arose as a topic of discussion.

5. Have several pointed questions to address to the whole group, if needed, to open the discussion. Never address questions to individual members unless it is to help them in what they are trying to say or to get them involved in the discussion.

6. Show appreciation for each member's contribution and personally reject no comment as incorrect or unworthy. If comments are weird or out of harmony with revealed truth, encourage the group to evaluate these comments by asking, "Do you agree?" or "What experience have others in the group had on this subject?"

7. Keep the discussion on the topic, but do not attempt to limit it in too rigid a manner. Restate issues to bring the discussion back to the question. The leader must be adept at sensing what is relevant.

8. Be equipped to take notes on the progress of the discussion, for these brief notes will be helpful in directing progress and making summaries.

9. Be sure that the discussion proceeds among the members of the class, not between the leader and successive members.

10. Close the meeting with a brief summary. Isolate valuable ideas, indicate progress in thinking, suggest the conclusions, decisions, or disagreements to which the class has come. Point up unsolved problems and unsettled issues.

11. Above all, attempt to end the discussion in good spirits and a desire for future experience with such a method.

The following questions may help the teacher evaluate his effectiveness in leading a discussion:

1. Did I state the problem clearly?

2. Did I challenge their thinking in setting forth the problem or issue?

3. Did the members of the group know they were expected to participate?

4. Did a few of the members dominate the discussion?

5. Was the group too large or too small? (The ideal number for informal discussion groups is somewhere between 8 and 20.)

6. Was the room comfortable and was everyone seated so that all could see and hear?

7. Did the discussion proceed among the members of the group?

8. Did I avert heated discussion by injecting humor or inserting a conciliatory word?

9. Did I summarize effectively?

A word of warning must be given at this point. Though the discussion is an effective means to adult learning, it is not a panacea for all adult education ills. Use informal discussion only when it appears to be the best teaching method under the existing circumstances.

Combinations of Lecture and Discussion

Frequently, the lecture and discussion techniques are combined effectively. A brief lecture, for example, may be followed by "buzz groups" or "huddles" in which groups of four or five members of the class discuss briefly certain phases of the lecture. These several groups then report back, to the total class, their findings or conclusions. Such combinations can be used with larger classes which are too unwieldy for informal discussion.

Other such combinations are . . .

The Panel Discussion

Using this method, the teacher and five to eight persons discuss, before the larger class, various aspects of the topic under study. After this period of discussion is completed, the leader summarizes and then invites questions or comments from the larger group. A final summary is then given.

The Forum Dialogue

This method is used when two persons who have studied the topic or subject carefully engage in dialogue—either question-and-answer, interview, or debate. Following this presentation, the two may answer questions from the floor, or the leader may direct a general discussion of ideas that grew out of the dialogue.

A Symposium

Several people speak for brief periods of time introducing several aspects of a given topic. When these have finished their presentations, discussion or questions may be called for from the larger group.

Seminars

Individual class members are given research assignments and they report on these assignments to the whole class. Questions can be addressed to them or a discussion can be conducted about some of the ideas presented.

Since many adult classes in our church schools are too large to carry on informal group discussion, these combination-type methods will prove helpful in conserving some of the values of the discussion method in less than ideal circumstances.

Research or Home Study Method

If the local church has adequate library resources, either in a public library or in its own church library, home study can be utilized effectively with adults. Properly challenged, adults will continue to learn and will even take initiative in learning. Teachers who are willing to take the time and expend the effort can work out home study projects, research problems, and outside readings that will correlate with the topics being studied in the Bible-school class. Those adults who take advantage of these opportunities could be asked to report on their reading and home study.

Projects

Someone has defined the project as "a problematical act carried to completion in its natural setting."

There are different types of projects in which any class might participate.[2] There are projects designed to secure information; projects that attempt to change or develop certain attitudes; and service projects in which needs are met by concerned Christians. Any of these can be used to reinforce what has been taught and to bring new facets of understanding and concern.

Here are four values of the project method:

1. The project makes learning more natural and interesting. The more concrete and meaningful learning experience is, the more effectively we learn.

2. The project gives basic training in initiative, responsibility, perseverance, foresight, alertness, judgment, and evaluation. The students themselves must be active and, under proper guidance, they will develop these characteristics as they engage in meaningful activity.

3. The project develops a spirit of cooperation. As committees or "task groups" are formed to work on certain aspects of the problem, cooperation is promoted and students learn to share out of their knowledge and ability.

4. The project fixes learning more clearly in the mind. That which we learn naturally we retain better. The boy who has learned to ride a bicycle by riding a bicycle (and by falling from time to time in those earlier attempts) never seems to forget what he has learned.

The following are limitations of the project method:

1. The project requires a teacher of superior skill who can

guide and inspire pupils to plan, execute, and evaluate the activity involved in carrying out the project.

2. The project runs the risk of overemphasizing mere physical activity. The old adage, "we learn by doing," needs to be changed to, "we learn through thinking about what we are purposively doing."

3. The project is time-consuming. Several class periods may be used to carry out a project to completion.

4. The project requires an eager and enthusiastic class. No project can be carried out when the majority of the class is indifferent or complacent.

5. The project demands adequate class space and facilities. If committees or groups work on various aspects of the project at the same time, enough room must be secured. If research is necessary, library resources will also be needed.

6. The project method may produce a situation where the individual may be overlooked. Individual students who are somewhat shy or backward could easily be ignored or bypassed as the project is carried out. After all, the project is supposed to be related to the needs and interests of the class. If it does not involve all members, it defeats its real purpose.

Other Methods

There are many other methods that can be used effectively with adults.

1. The question-and-answer method has real merit as thought-provoking questions are devised to promote thinking and to initiate discussion.

2. The story method, though frequently limited to childhood education, is still effective with older students as well.

3. Visuals have come to the front in recent years because of the advances that have been made in machines and because of the benefit that such visual presentations have produced in education. Experiments have indicated that we learn better when visually stimulated. Projected and non-projected visuals are based solidly upon this fact and have been used effectively in adult education.

Non-projected visuals include pictures, maps, chalk talks, chalkboard studies, charts, graphs, and objects of all sorts. These aids are used in conjunction with lectures, discussions, projects, or other such methods. They illustrate, explain, summarize, or clarify that which is under discussion.

Projected visuals, such as filmstrips, slides, or moving pictures, are somewhat more complicated than the non-projected visual aids.

In some instances tapes or records are used with films to make the impact that much more effective. These projected visuals should be used correctly to produce the most benefit. The class should be prepared for visuals by suggesting what they ought to be looking for or by asking them to identify themselves with certain of the characters in the film. The visual should be followed by class discussion. The discussion or question-and-answer method could be used. Visuals, particularly projected visuals, can become monotonous through overuse. Here, as elsewhere, teachers need to strive for variety.

Role-playing is an effective way of gaining insight into the problems of others. It is a method in which a real-life situation is posed. Members of the class are asked to assume different character roles suggested in the situation. Without developing a dramatic script, rehearsal, or memorizing lines, these class members spontaneously act out the situation. The value of this approach is that individual members gain insight of the problems, attitudes, and thinking of others. It is most beneficial when a skillful teacher is able to so understand his pupils that he can arrange the role-play so that the pupil will play a role which is opposite of his own real-life role. Understanding is thus developed and prejudices can be broken down.

Role-playing requires an imaginative group as well as a certain amount of planning and direction on the part of the teacher or leader. It is limited in use to problem areas of teaching and, undoubtedly, is most effective when used infrequently.

Summary

We have seen in this chapter that the teacher may use a wide variety of methods in presenting the lesson material. While we have cautioned the teacher against using methods in which he has not developed skill, we have sought to encourage him to work with diligence to develop skill in new methods. The most significant point to remember regarding methods is this, no matter what the method is, it should not be used exclusively. Finally, the effective teacher will always be on the lookout for ways to improve the various methods he employs.

Books for Further Study

CALDWELL, IRENE S. *Adults Learn and Like It*. Anderson, Indiana: Warner Press, 1955.

CLEMMONS, ROBERT S. *Dynamics of Adult Education*. New York: Abingdon Press, 1958. Chapter V.

EDGE, FINDLEY B. *Helping the Teacher.* Nashville: Broadman Press, 1959.

KNOWLES, MALCOLM S. *Informal Adult Education.* New York: Association Press, 1950.

LENTZ, RICHARD E. *Making the Adult Class Vital.* St. Louis: Bethany Press, 1954. Chapter VI.

LINDHORST, FRANK A. *Teaching Adults.* New York: Abingdon Press, 1951.

McKINLEY, JOHN. *Creative Methods for Adult Classes.* St. Louis: Bethany Press, 1960.

MILLER, RANDOLPH CRUMP. *Education for Christian Living.* Englewood Cliffs, New Jersey: Prentice-Hall, Inc., 1956. Part III.

Questions for Discussion

1. What were the two most common teaching methods prior to the twentieth century?

2. Discuss the characteristics of some of the newer teaching methods. '

3. Name five important factors .to be considered in selecting the most effective teaching method for a given situation.

4. What can a teacher do to create discussion in a class that tends to be indifferent?

5. Discuss ways a teacher could develop skill in the use of new methods.

6. Discuss the advantages of the lecture method.

7. Show how a competent teacher can overcome many of the weaknesses of the lecture method.

8. Why is the teacher or leader the key to an effective use of the discussion method?

9. Suggest several topics that could be handled effectively in an adult class by the discussion method.

10. Suggest ways the research method could be combined with the lecture or discussion methods.

NOTES

[1] Findley B. Edge, *Helping the Teacher* (Nashville: Broadman Press, 1959), p. 86.
[2] *Ibid,* pp. 142-144.

CHAPTER 8

The Curriculum for Adults

Curriculum materials are an important part of a successful adult class. We shall never reach the desired goals in Christian education if we make lightly our choice of study materials.

The History of Curriculum

Limiting our historical survey to American education we find that the curriculum materials of the colonial period were catechisms based upon creeds and confessional standards. The systematic plan was to use these in a rigid, authoritarian manner with a view to developing the ability of the student to memorize and repeat back the questions and answers found in the catechisms. By about 1820 the Sunday school had become the chief agency of religious education among American denominations. Due to the great emphasis upon the Bible, in many cases the curriculum materials had been changed from catechism to the Scriptures. The systematic plan, however, continued to involve memorization, drill, and recitation with no real attempt to relate such a program to meaningfulness and relevance to everyday life.

Prior to and following the Civil War, attempts were made to provide a different kind of curriculum material for the Sunday schools of America. Different men in different areas began publishing lesson helps and designating courses of study from Biblical materials. Because these were so varied in nature and vied with each other for support, this period is often called the "Babel" period in the development of American Sunday School curriculum materials. Though none of these "plans" succeeded, they did call attention to the need for designating areas to be studied and providing comments, helps, and ideas for those who would teach. These "plans" prepared the way for both the "uniform" and "graded" series that soon developed.

In 1872 the International Sunday School Convention approved a lesson committee to work out a Uniform Lesson System. The idea was that one lesson series could be devised which all Sunday schools in America could study at the same time, thus producing unity in the Sunday-school ranks and making for better preparation of teachers. Publishers, then, could provide commentaries, lesson helps, and aids for this one uniform lesson each week. Attempts were made to grade or adapt each week's lesson to younger children; however, this did not prove too successful and this weakness became apparent in the Uniform series.

The International Sunday School Association, which grew out of the International Convention, soon was besieged by children's workers to do something about curricular materials for elementary students. By 1900 the understanding of psychological development of the individual had developed to the point that grading systems were created and specific materials prepared for specific age groups were demanded. In 1906 a close-graded series was developed by the Association and in 1924 a cycle-graded series was approved.

Besides these programs and materials sponsored by the International Sunday School Association on an interdenominational basis, the National Sunday School Association also provides the Uniform Bible Lesson Series. Certain religious groups, notably the Lutherans and Congregationalists, have developed graded curriculums for their own constituency.

At the present the curriculum situation is quite complex. Besides the Uniform Lessons, which are now sponsored by the Division of Christian Education of the National Council of Churches of Christ in America and which are used by almost every religious group in America in some way, there are almost as many graded systems as there are denominational or independent publishers. The trend is toward emphasizing graded materials at every level (with perhaps the exception of adults) and to urge every church school to use such graded materials. The Uniform Lessons, however, still remain popular in some churches and with the young people and adult age groups.

Factors in Selecting Curriculum

1. *The first factor to keep in mind in selecting curriculum material is that the Bible is the foundation for all study material.* The Bible must be considered our sole and all-sufficient source and authority for all matters pertaining to religion. Its message defines our faith, establishes our doctrines, and directs our practices. We live by its standards, we accept its terms of salvation, and we base our hopes upon its promises. Because of these facts the Bible of necessity becomes the foundation of all our curriculum materials. It is debatable whether or not any curriculum material has a place in our adult Sunday-school class which does not either explain the Bible or help us put its teachings into practice.

2. *A second factor to be considered is the nature and needs of the people in the class.* We have the guidelines of understanding the nature of human life in the Bible, but curriculum materials must present these truths in a manner the pupil can comprehend. Within a class there are pupils in various stages of spiritual development. The selection of materials for study must meet the needs of the majority of these pupils. There will arise from time to time special needs of both individuals and classes. The curriculum must be flexible enough to allow special studies to meet these needs.

3. *A third factor to be considered in selecting curriculum material is the purpose of the church.* The church of the New Testament was a community of faith. It was an evangelizing association in its entirety. It was a fellowship of persons who were aware they had been called out of the world to a life of holiness. It was a group of people in need of growing in grace and knowledge of Jesus Christ. It was an organism that worshiped, served, and leavened its society. The church today should select curriculum materials that will create the same kind of program and produce the same kind of people. Every congregation should objectively appraise the effect its teaching and teaching materials are having upon its people. If it discovers it is not fulfilling its divine purpose and its people are not to some degree emulating the example of the New Testament church, a part of the problem may rest in the curriculum materials that are being used.

4. *The factor of educational philosophy must also be considered in the selection of curriculum materials.* If one is committed to a philosophy of naturalism and behavioristic psychology, he will likely select materials that consider learning to be purely mechanistic. Such a philosophy advocates social reform without emphasis upon the regeneration of the individual. It contends the individual is fully capable of setting his own moral standards without consideration of divine revelation. It discounts the reality of sin and Satan. And it regards the Bible as but one of many sources of moral teaching.

On the other hand, if one believes in God as the Creator and ruler of the universe, accepts the Bible as His inspired revelation, and considers the Bible to be the supreme and final authority in all matters of faith and conduct, he will want curriculum materials that uphold this concept.

Other aspects of educational philosophy can be seen in a publisher's approach to learning. Some materials are prepared with a complete emphasis on content. Facts are stated in a cold and impersonal manner. They are to be taught and accepted in a catechistic way. Such an approach does not necessarily uphold the Bible as authoritative nor does it give proper consideration to the individual's need or reaction. If learning could be assured through exposure to factual data, this philosophy might be valid, but this is not always the case.

Other materials are completely pupil-centered. When this philosophy is embraced, the materials are presented with the assumption that man is good and he can lift himself unassisted. Such a philosophy gives the pupil the final judgment as to what is learned and as to what can be learned. It assumes man can find from within the information he needs in life. Such materials are usually prepared to appeal to popular whims and unduly exalt the value of sharing ideas in group discussion. Also, such materials constantly stress understanding the pupil and give little regard for the content of the lesson material.

The preferred materials are those that are Bible-based, Christ-centered, and pupil-directed. Materials prepared by publishers who hold to this philosophy will make the Bible facts the basis of each lesson. Sufficient treatment will be given to the Bible passage to assure understanding. Christ and Christianity will shine through as the central theme of all lesson materials. In the lesson application consideration will be given to making it relevant to the age group for which it is prepared. And finally, the materials will be prepared in such a way that a variety of teaching methods can be employed to maintain the maximum interest level.

5. *Still another factor to consider in selecting curriculum material is theology.* The church must be concerned about what it teaches. The theology presented in its literature in reality becomes its teaching. Most teachers as well as pupils of adult classes are novices in theology and will therefore accept unquestioned what appears in their literature. Because of this fact the selection of curriculum materials that do not contain false doctrines becomes a crucial point. Materials also should be avoided that are so general they produce no convictions. The final test in theology should be, "Are the materials true to the Bible?"

6. *Finally, the factor of design should be considered when selecting curriculum materials for adults.* Within the principle of design are the subprinciples of sequence and flexibility. By sequence is meant that there is noticeable progression in the materials which guide a student toward maturity in Christ. By flexibility is meant that the curriculum materials are so designed that they allow for individual and cultural differences, and they can be adapted by creative teachers to different contexts and conditions. This factor

reminds us that no curriculum materials are perfect in design. They all must be adapted by the teacher and the pupil to local and individual needs. The point is, "Were they designed in such a way that the adaptation can be made?"

Types of Curriculum Materials

Uniform Lessons. Uniform Lessons have been quite popular with adults almost from their inception. Arising out of a deep need in 1872, they have been published continuously since that time. The outlines, through the years, have been worked out by a representative lesson committee appointed first by the International Sunday School Convention, later the International Sunday School Association and the International Council of Religious Education. It is now the Division of Christian Education of the National Council of Churches of Christ in America. These are now called the "International Bible Lessons for Christian Teaching, Uniform Series" and are described as a "system of lessons, biblical in content, maintaining the principle of uniformity through including a core of common material and emphasis to be developed in all age groups, but providing for a graded approach through supplemental materials and adaptations within the several age groups."

The Uniform Lessons are set up in a cycle of six years in which an historical coverage of the entire Bible is attempted along with emphasis upon Christian growth, Bible doctrines, and ethical problems. The general structure of the cycle can be observed by using the 1963-1968 series as an example. In four years of the cycle the first quarter of each year is given to a study of the life of Christ. In the remaining two years during this quarter one year is given to a study of personalities around Christ and the other to a study of major doctrines of the Christian faith. The spring and summer quarters are given to a study of the historical portions of the Bible. The fall quarters are devoted to studies of the New Testament writings other than the Gospels and Acts, and to the prophets and other outstanding personalities of the Old Testament. The entire cycle contains 130 lessons from the Old Testament and 183 based on the New Testament.

Because the Uniform Lessons are Biblical in nature and emphasize uniformity, many adults prefer them. There is also some merit in having the entire family considering the same portion of Scripture in their Bible study. Others, however, do not care for the fragmentary treatment of the Biblical material and this type of topical arrangement.

Graded Lessons. Since grading is a matter of controversy with

67

adults, Graded lesson materials for them are almost nonexistent. As long as there is no consensus as to whether adults should be grouped according to age, sex, or interests, no satisfactory system of graded lessons can be worked out.

One possible approach to adult Graded Lessons might be to develop a cycle of lessons covering the areas of basic needs among adults. This material would then be offered in such a way as to require adults to take certain "core" courses, adding to them electives related to their individual interest.

Elective studies. Some churches have introduced the "elective plan" in their Adult Departments. Using this plan, courses of varying lengths and academic levels are offered. Usually the adults are permitted to select the course of their choice, one option being the Uniform Lesson series.

There are several disadvantages in this type of curriculum. One is that the selection of courses may not be educationally sound. Courses may be chosen on the basis of the likes or dislikes of the minister, teacher, or some other individual in the church. If this person does not know how to develop a curriculum, there is the danger of having an excessive amount of study in some areas and a complete negligence of others. There is also the tendency to overlook correlation. Another problem in following exclusively the elective system of studies is the amount of material available. On the surface it would appear there is an abundance of material available, but when one tries to arrange it into a correlated curriculum he may find inadequacies. A further problem regarding materials is the fact that they may not be prepared as well as they should be for general classroom usage.

Elective studies do have merit when properly used. They can be very effective when used in conjunction with a "core" of basic lesson materials. They are highly desirable to meet special needs that arise in the class. An elective study is needed when one desires to use a special emphasis throughout the church for a given period of time.

May we emphasize again that the curriculum for an adult class must be devised. No single type of curriculum materials is the perfect answer.

Workbook studies. This type of curriculum material is prepared on a selected topic or as a study of a certain portion of the Bible. The material is prepared in the form of questions and answers. Space is usually left for the pupil to write in the correct answer to the questions asked after he has read the suggested passage in the Bible. Such studies are very popular in some adult classes. The workbook type study has several points in its favor. First, it gets the pupils involved in the study of the lesson. Second, the contents of a workbook study are usually simple enough to be understood by anyone. A third advantage is that the answers desired are specific, and the adult has no fear of giving the wrong answer. A fourth factor in their favor is the fact they often ask the same questions that have been in the mind of the pupil. When the pupil can get an answer for his questions from the Bible, he receives a sense of satisfaction.

There are also some unfavorable factors about workbook studies. First, their rigid style tends to be monotonous when used over a long period of time. Second, they limit the teacher in the use of teaching methods. Third, a pupil may mechanically look up the answer to a question and write an answer down without having a learning experience. Fourth, the author of the workbook may misuse the Bible as prooftexts for his bias. Fifth, the materials may be purely factual and they may overlook the important element of application.

Therefore, the workbook should not be avoided, but on the other hand it should not be considered as the ultimate in curriculum materials.

Verse-by-verse Bible study. This approach to study materials can help to eliminate the danger of always studying about the Bible instead of studying the Bible itself. If such a study is led by a qualified teacher, and if the passages for study are carefully selected, this type of study has certain advantages over other types of study. However, it does not automatically solve all curriculum problems. For example, if a class stays in a study of a given book for a long period of time, interest may lag and other important subject matter may be neglected. Sometimes when this type of study is used, the pupil is provided no resource material for personal enlightenment. Nearly always such studies tend to emphasize content and neglect application. When verse-by-verse studies are not carefully selected the Christian education needs of the majority of the class may not be met.

In 1965 a report was issued following an extensive survey by sixteen denominations on the subject of curriculum development. The results of this survey showed that in the final analysis the responsibility for the development of an adequate curriculum lies first upon the local congregation. The church that will take seriously its responsibility in this matter will select its curriculum materials only after careful planning and thorough investigation of the materials available.

69

Books for Further Study

BETTS, GEORGE H. *The Curriculum of Religious Education.* New York: Abingdon Press, 1924.

BOWER, W. C. *The Curriculum of Religious Education.* New York: Charles Scribner's Sons, 1925.

The Curriculum Design for Christian Education, 6 vols. Lutheran Board of Parish Education, 1960-62.

Curriculum Guide for the Local Church. Chicago: International Council of Religious Education, 1950.

LENTZ, RICHARD E. *Making the Adult Class Vital.* St. Louis: Bethany Press, 1954.

WYCKOFF, D. CAMPBELL. *Theory and Design of Christian Education Curriculum.* Philadelphia: Westminster Press, 1961.

Questions for Discussion

1. Discuss the curriculum materials used in America during the colonial period.

2. What was the idea behind the Uniform Lesson system?

3. What is the current status of Graded Sunday-school materials?

4. Name the six factors to be considered in selecting curriculum materials.

5. What is meant by curriculum materials that are content-centered?

6. Why is it important to know the theology of publishers of curriculum materials?

7. Discuss the advantages and disadvantages of the Uniform Lesson materials.

8. How can a church devise the best curriculum for its Adult Department?

CHAPTER 9

Beyond the Classroom

Christian education must always be seen as including other activities in addition to formal instruction. Service projects, purposeful activities, meaningful worship, and expressions of group fellowship are all involved in Christian education. A total program of adult education for the church must provide experiences of sharing and learning in these significant areas of church life.

Worship and Adult Education

The church, basically, is a worshiping community. No other aspect of its life is more in keeping with its basic nature. We are redeemed and reconciled in order that we may be properly related to the living God. In worship we express the new relationship we enjoy in the redeemed community.

What do we mean by worship? The word "worship" is derived from the Middle English *worschipe,* which in turn is from the Anglo-Saxon *wearthscipe* which means "worthship." Worship of God, then, is declaring God's worth or value. It involves a subjective attitude of reverence and awe toward Him who is Creator, Lord, and Saviour. It involves an objective expression in word and deed indicative of an attitude and relationship of dependence. As the Westminster Shorter Catechism states it: "The chief end of man is to glorify God and enjoy Him forever."

Involved in New Testament worship are several elements, although no clean-cut worship service is to be found in which all these elements are included or related in an orderly fashion. Prayer was essential to the life of the early Christian community (Acts 2:42; 12:5,12) since it expressed so intimately that communion enjoyed by every Christian with the Most High God. Singing, apparently, was considered significant for both private and public worship (Colossians 3:16; Ephesians 5:19; Acts 16:25; 1 Corinthians 14:26). Paul indicates that the act of giving may be seen as a part of corporate worship (1 Corinthians 16:1, 2). The apostles' teaching, either in instruction or in sermon, was also a part of those activities in which the early church engaged as they worshiped (Acts 2:42; Acts 20:7; 1 Corinthians 14:24, 26). In New Testa-

71

ment worship the celebration of the Lord's Supper was most significant. This was the basic purpose for the church gathering together at Troas (Acts 20:7), and apparently the reason for the Corinthian church to come together (1 Corinthians 11:17-34). Historically, the church has recognized this basic Biblical emphasis—the centrality of the Lord's Supper—though it distorted the initial significance of this single ceremony through medieval accretions and changes. Through the Lord's Supper with its focus upon God's action in Christ; through the Word with its emphasis upon God's self-disclosure; through songs of praise directed toward the Creator of the universe; and through prayer arising in reverent hearts and addressed to the Lord of hosts, worship is seen as God-centered not man-centered, as objective responsible expression and not mere subjective, emotional satisfaction.[1]

The educational implications of worship. Worship is not only educational, it provides the "framework in which Christian education takes place, for in worship the believing community is in communion with God, who provides the redemption that the community needs. Without the means of grace vouchsafed through worship, education is likely to founder on the rocks of factual knowledge, moralism, and loyalty to the church as an idolatrous end in itself."[2] Worship as a framework for Christian education not only undergirds the educational task but enervates and energizes the educational process. We educate in Christian truth and Christian living in order that a closer relationship between God and man might be known, and this relationship will always be expressed in our worship. Vital worship, then, will become one of the means of ascertaining whether we are really educating our people.

Other educational implications of worship are seen as we look at the various elements of active worship. The "preaching of the word" is educative; it is the wisdom of God that brings salvation (1 Corinthians 1:24). The Word presents facts to be believed, commands to be obeyed, warnings to be heeded, and promises to be enjoyed. This process is educational. It may be primarily designed to change the will and elicit decisions, but it is nevertheless educational.

Prayer has important educational overtones. "Teach us to pray," was requested by the disciples. Prayer, to be effective, must be taught. Though it appears to be spontaneous at times, such apparent spontaneity is seen only in lives where the discipline of prayer has been most effective. We shall pray intelligently only when we have been taught what prayer is all about.

Giving involves education and instruction as is indicated by Paul's instructions and exhortations to the Corinthians (1 Corinthians 9; 2 Corinthians 8, 9). Jesus had much to teach about the importance of giving and the insidious danger of covetousness. The intelligent contribution of funds as a partial expression of our stewardship is a response which can be taught. At this point worship and Christian education are integrally related.

The Lord's Supper stands as a central act of worship. In the object lesson impressed upon the mind by the bread and the cup there is teaching which can constantly remind us of God's gracious action in and through Jesus Christ. There must be instruction as to the significance of this observance because the observance itself dramatically presents to all who are spiritually apprehensive the true nature of the gospel (1 Corinthians 15:1-3; 1 Corinthians 11: 17 ff.). In this very act we "shew the Lord's death till he come" (1 Corinthians 11:26).

Worship provides the framework for education within the church and education reciprocates by training worshipers in more effective worship. The two cannot be successfully severed.

Planning adult worship. The worship experiences provided for adults both in the worship hour and in connection with other activities ought to be meaningful and uplifting. Too often, within the Bible-school period, worship is limited to an "opening exercise" which (as someone has well said) neither opens anything nor exercises anything. Such opening worship is seldom related to the class period following and is often rushed through so that we can get at the more important matter of formal instruction.

We must learn to worship through worshiping. "Worship, whether it takes place in a family service, departmental assembly, or classroom, is experience-centered education, for the worshiper learns by doing." [3] Therefore, adults should be encouraged to participate actively in every phase of worship provided by the church. The church and the church school should so plan worship experiences to allow for meaningful participation. Such things as congregational singing, responsive reading of the Scriptures, the opportunity to give, and time for silent prayer, can become a part of meaningful worship.

Adults should also come to appreciate the value of family worship. They should be encouraged to inaugurate some type of worship in their own homes. Through such experiences the family is knit together in a common bond, and children become aware, almost from birth, of the significance of God in their lives.

Adults should also cooperate with the Bible school in its attempt to provide worship experiences for children's departments and classes. If worship is a learned experience, it must be learned at the level of the individual who is learning. Too often, the public worship service is adult-centered and adult-oriented. The value of extended sessions and graded worship for children should be given a hearing by adults.

The adult teachers must set the pattern. They must be aware that God is constantly at work in human life. They must be able to speak of spiritual things in a realistic, nonembarrassed manner. They must set the tone in prayer and other participative acts of worship. At this point, religion may be "caught" more than "taught."

Weekly officers' and teachers' meetings can be inaugurated to provide help both administratively and educationally for teachers and officers of the Bible school. Educational features relating to departmental work, teaching methods for the particular age group, or a demonstration of how to teach a lesson for the coming Sunday could be a part of such meetings. They can be an invaluable tool for preparing better teachers.[4]

Workers' conferences, regularly scheduled, with careful planning of the program will also aid in leadership training for Bible-school workers. If there is no weekly officers' and teachers' meeting, the workers' conference could include educational features as well as matters of an administrative and organizational nature.

Responsibility could also be placed upon the individual leader by encouraging personal study in areas of special interest. The ideal adult church leader engages in continuous study and growth. He is anxious for leadership training. To cultivate this interest an adequate church library and the proper guidance of some knowledgeable leader will be needed. Every effort should be made to see that potential leaders study from proper sources and according to some plan.

In-service or apprentice training can also be encouraged. All Bible-school teachers and workers should have assistants who participate actively in the program and are called upon to serve regularly. These assistants should be enlisted, recruited, and involved in some of the above activities of leadership education. What is true of the Bible school is also true of other areas of educational life in the church.

These programs are but suggestions as to the development of an adult program of leadership education. The main task is to prepare leaders and teachers who are able "to teach others also" (2 Timothy 2:2). The general program of spiritual education in the church depends upon the effectiveness with which we accomplish this task.

Fellowship Activities and Adult Education

The meaning of fellowship. Fellowship, understood in the New Testament sense, is that partnership in which all Christians participate with Jesus Christ. It includes every phase of our common life in Christ, through the church. It is not merely a back-slapping, hilarious period of festive fun. It includes sociability, but it goes beyond this to include every other phase of Christian life and activity. There are, however, activities related to man's sociability and his need for recreation which can promote fellowship.

Man is essentially gregarious; he wants companionship, social relationship, and opportunities for cooperative endeavor. A social or recreational committee of the Adult Department or class should plan and execute activities that will meet man's social needs and promote spiritual fellowship.

Fellowship activities. In an excellent work, *Recreation and the Local Church,* by Clemens, Tully, and Crill, a chapter is devoted to "Recreation and the Age Groups." Excellent recreational suggestions are made for each area of adult life. Family recreation is also encouraged. The local church is clearly challenged to provide for these needs by study, promotion, and the creation of some kind of committee to provide direction in meeting these needs. This book (and others suggested at the close of this chapter) could be studied and used with profit by those concerned with these problems.

The activities, however, with which we are most concerned are those that promote fellowship. The basic purpose of these activities is to provide a creative outlet for adults through participation. It may be difficult to achieve this purpose at first; for most adults, even in church recreation, settle "for an occasional dinner out and some sort of vicarious experience rather than for participation." [5] However, if the committee will do adequate planning, offer a Christian basis for its recreation, and provide variety in activities, adults will respond.

Irene Smith Caldwell suggests the following qualities to look for in that creative recreation that should be planned for adults:

1. It provides for a maximum of participation.
2. It is genuinely interesting.
3. It is fun and can be continued through life.
4. It provides the opportunity for individuality.
5. It is thought provoking.
6. It releases physical energy and emotions.
7. It provides opportunity for human associations and recognition.
8. It provides for self-expression and balance.
9. It opens a variety of new interests.
10. It leads to social sensitiveness and co-operation. [6]

Within the scope of activities that could be provided for adults are parties, game nights, picnics, retreats, camping experiences, provision for hobbies and crafts, dramatic programs, music and reading sessions. These should be varied throughout the year, with the season setting the pattern for the kind of activity and the possible theme of the social.

Planning social recreation. Activities do not just happen, they are planned, and the people who shall participate must be prepared. Hence, committee members whose job it is to develop a social program for the Bible-school class or department ought to be chosen with care. Such members should be creative, have unbounded enthusiasm, and have a sound philosophy of the importance of recreation in the lives of people.

The planning process should include overall planning for the year. A calendar of recreational and social events can be developed as a guide. Some fellowship activity should be planned for each month. A variety of activities and seasonal themes should be projected in these overall plans. The general recreation committee may wish to appoint other committees to be responsible for the monthly activity. At least, there ought to be an involvement of other people in some phase of the planning and preparation of each activity. Provision of decorations, invitations, refreshments, etc., provide opportunities for involving a number of adults each month.

Planning the actual program of the social event is most important. The various phases or divisions of the program need adequate preparation. A central theme should be chosen and the various sections of the social should relate to this theme (such books as listed at the close of this chapter will be helpful sources). Planned activities for early arrivals should not be overlooked, for "getting people off to a good start is ninety percent of the struggle." [7] Informal *"ice-breakers" or "mixers" functions* will get the individuals acquainted and participating together. These should never require so much skill that people hesitate to participate. Often they will relate to learning names or getting better acquainted with those they already know by name. Various *types of games*— both active and quiet, both manual and intellectual—will make up the body of the program. Skillful balance between these types of activities should be sought. *Refreshments* can be included in the body of the program with other games or activities following, rather than at the end of the social as has been customary. Such a plan integrates the refreshment time into the total program as a quiet participation and allows the program to build to a climax in some kind of worship experience.

The committee's job is not over with the washing of the dishes used for refreshments. Evaluation needs to be made of the social event shortly afterwards. Such questions as, What activity did the participants enjoy most? Why? Did the social accomplish its purpose? What weaknesses were apparent? Such an analysis and evaluation will make for better social events in the future.

Missions and Adult Education

The church's mission is missions; or, to put it another way, evangelism at home and abroad. Yet, so frequently, missions are limited to a women's missionary society or to some kind of impersonal allocation of funds from the church's budget. This ought not to be. The total church should be a missionary organization with every age and group involved in mission study and activity.

Every adult class and/or department should be vitally interested in the extension of Christ's kingdom both at home and abroad. A few minutes' time spent each Sunday in study about and prayer for those who labor in the various mission fields can contribute greatly to the general understanding and missionary education of each adult member. A missionary committee of the class could constantly be searching for new ways to introduce the subject of missions into the class session. Prayer calendars, maps, news flashes, current events—all could be used for this purpose.

Missionary projects. Nothing interests people more than those matters in which they are personally involved and for which they have expended time and effort. The mission committee might well suggest some project or projects that the class could carry out. Used clothing drives, monthly financial support, and other such projects for both home and foreign missionaries or agencies would be worthy projects. Community service projects in the local area could also be accepted. Helping the poor or the underprivileged in one's community often will be the foundation of a mission Sunday school or Vacation Bible School as a real challenge and make this a continuous project. Other classes might consider the beginning of a day camp for needy youngsters or the development of a weekday Christian education program as a worthy project. Any class or department that will give some creative thought to the matter will find more projects than they can possibly undertake.

Outreach. An active Bible school will be constantly seeking to enlist more people. It must always be concerned with outreach. Therefore, every class should be seeking to reach all those in its community who are unreached. This outreach involves:

1. *Discovering prospects.* This can be done through conducting a periodic census, following up on visitors who attend the church's services, checking on prospects enlisted in the Vacation Bible School, and pursuing every lead found in utility reports, "welcome wagon" information, newspapers, and business contacts.

2. *Establishing and maintaining regular contact.* When prospects are discovered, they should be visited with a view to establishing a warm, friendly relationship between them and the church. This relationship must be maintained, even when the prospects remain unenlisted and do not attend.

3. *Enrolling persons in Sunday school.* Outreach should result in enrollment in and attendance of the class sessions of the Bible school.

4. *Visitation.* Enrollment in a Sunday-school class is not enough. Besides the Bible-teaching and evangelistic emphasis presented in the classroom, there must also be continued visitation with a view to winning these people to Christ and to His church.

Outreach, then, involves visitation, and every adult member of every Bible-school class should actively engage in such visitation. This is missions at a personal level. Each adult member can be involved in such missionary endeavor.

Conclusion

Worship, fellowship, activities, and missionary emphases and projects are vital aspects of the church's total program. They are directly related to the Bible-school program for adults. Such "beyond the classroom" activities must be implemented by concerted action. May each Adult Department or class develop ways and means of involving its membership in those activities which will extend the kingdom of Jesus Christ and promote fellowship among those who are redeemed.

Books for Further Study

CALDWELL, IRENE. *Responsible Adults in the Church School Program.* Anderson, Indiana: The Warner Press, 1961.

CARLSON, ADELLE. *Four Seasons Party and Banquet Book.* Nashville: Broadman Press.

CLEMENS, FRANCES, ROBERT TULLY, and EDWARD CRILL. *Recreation and the Local Church.* Elgin, Illinois: Brethren Publishing House, 1956.

DEPEW, ARTHUR M. *The Cokesbury Party Book* (rev. ed.). Nashville: Abingdon Press, 1959.

————. *The Cokesbury Game Book* (rev. ed.). Nashville: Abingdon Press.

EISENBERG, HELEN AND LARRY. *The Family Fun Book.* New York: Association Press.

GWYNN, PRICE H., JR. *Leadership Education in the Local Church.* Philadelphia: The Westminster Press, 1952.

HARBIN, ELVIN O. *Fun Encyclopedia.* New York: Abingdon-Cokesbury.

_____. *The Recreation Leader.* New York: Abingdon Press, 1952.

HARNER AND BAKER. *Missionary Education in the Local Church.* New York: Friendship Press.

HOWSE, W. L. *The Sunday School and Missions.* Nashville: Convention Press.

LAMBDIN, J. E. *Building a Church Training Program.* Nashville: Convention Press, 1946.

MCKIBBEN, FRANK M. *Guiding Workers in Christian Education.* Nashville: Abingdon Press, 1947.

MURCH, JAMES DEFOREST. *Christian Education and the Local Church* (rev. ed.). Cincinnati: Standard Publishing, 1958.

PYLANT, AGNES DURANT. *Fun Plans for Church Recreation.* Nashville: Broadman Press, 1958.

Questions for Discussion

1. Define worship.

2. Name three elements that are evident in the worship services of the New Testament church.

3. Choose a phase of worship and discuss its educational implications.

4. Plan an adult worship service that can be used in an opening assembly of Sunday school in the Adult Department.

5. Give three reasons why adult classes should plan social activities.

6. What is the meaning of fellowship as it is used in the New Testament?

7. Why do missions have a place in every adult class?

8. Devise a plan of visitation for the Adult Department of which you are a member or of the class which you teach.

NOTES

[1] An excellent study of the "New Testament Concept of Worship" is to be found in the *Shane Quarterly*, Vol. 7, No. 3 (July, 1946), written by Dr. James G. VanBuren.

[2] Randolph C. Miller, *Education for Christian Living* (Englewood Cliffs, New Jersey: Prentice-Hall, Inc.), pp. 261, 262.

[3] *Ibid.*, p. 245.

[4] See *The Weekly Officers and Teachers' Meeting* Filmstrip (Nashville: Broadman Films).

[5] Irene S. Caldwell, *Responsible Adults in the Church School Program* (Anderson, Indiana: Warner Press), p. 83. Used by permission.

[6] *Ibid.*, p. 84.

[7] Frances Clemens, Robert Tully, and Edward Crill, *Recreation and the Local Church* (Elgin, Illinois: Brethren Publishing House, 1956), p. 157.

CHAPTER 10

Organizing Adults

Before discussing ways and means of organizing adults for effective growth and action, attention should be given to different concepts of organization. Webster defines organization as "that arrangement or constitution of any entity into interdependent parts, each having a special function, act, office, or relation with respect to the whole." Coleridge says, "Organization is but the connection of parts in and for a whole, so that each part is, at once, end and means." Someone has suggested this simple definition of organization: it is "to get into working order." From these definitions it is evident that we should not think of organization as mere mechanics but as a means of reaching our spiritual aims and objectives in the Adult Department. The purpose of adequate organization is therefore to produce a functioning church to be used of God to accomplish His will.

Grouping or Grading Adults

There are at least three possible ways to group the adults of the church into an effective program of learning and activities.

1. *Grading according to age.* Using this pattern departments and classes would be developed for young adults (25-35); middle-aged adults (36-55); and older adults (56 and up). There is very little argument against grading children or youth according to age, but there are some problems in grading adults by this method.

One of the most serious problems in using a grading system for adults based on age is the fact that not all adults in a given age bracket have a similar spiritual maturity. Those who are on different levels of spiritual maturity will need a different curriculum.

2. *Grading according to interests.* This system recommends adults be graded according to such things as interests, occupations, and environments. Using this system there would be a class for such groups as business and professional men and women, young married couples, homemakers, and college students. This system of grading would, of course, work best in a metropolitan center where there would be a good cross-section of interests and occupations.

3. *Grading according to elective subject matter.* Under this sys-

tem a well-balanced curriculum is developed. Adults of all ages are permitted to go to the class of their choice. Counsel can be given in assisting the adults to enroll in the class that would be most helpful to them in their particular level of spiritual development. To promote the benefits of fellowship, each of these classes could have a social committee to plan specific functions for the group.

It is impossible to say that either of these three systems are completely right or completely wrong. Each church must consider these and other means of grading adults. In most cases a combination of the above three types of grading is being used. Whatever system is used, the church should attempt to create groups who are like-minded, homogeneous, and who create an atmosphere for learning.

Guidelines for Organization

Dr. J. D. Murch suggests that organization should be devised along the guidelines suggested by four questions:

1. Is it *Scriptural* in principle?
2. Is it *simple*—without "fifth wheels" and "excess baggage"?
3. Is it *adequate*—fully discharging all necessary functions?
4. Is it *practical*—meeting the peculiar needs of the particular church and community in which it is located?[1]

Within the adult educational program of every church there is a need for a graded organization in which plans are made for all age groups. There is also a need for an administrative organization which provides leadership and direction for the total program. There must also be functional organization by which provision is made for the total needs of each person. Within the framework of all of this planning, one simple rule should be kept in mind—the least organization necessary to get the job done is the best.

Departmental Organization

In a large church where there are multiple adult classes it may be advisable to organize the Adult Department the same way in which the children or youth departments are organized. In such a case there would be a general superintendent for the Adult Department and several departmental superintendents serving under him. The departmental superintendent's responsibility would include seeing that each class had a teacher, that proper records were kept in each class, and directing the general assembly for the department where such was desirable.

In the smaller school there may be only two or three classes for adults. In such circumstances the general superintendent usually acts as the superintendent for the Adult Department. His responsibilities under this set-up include directing the assembly program, securing teachers for the various classes, and seeing that a high grade of Bible teaching is carried on in each class. Usually when this system is used the officers of the individual classes in conjunction with the teacher plan and expedite the social and service activities.

Both the general superintendent and the departmental superintendent should be well-qualified by temperament and training to provide leadership for the Adult Department.

Organizing the Adult Class

Not only does the Adult Department need adequate organization, each adult class also needs to be organized. Through class organization such matters as class projects, social affairs, visitation, and special church-wide activities can be handled.

Most classes organize in the *traditional* manner with a president, vice-president, secretary, and treasurer. The duties of the president are to preside over class sessions, business meetings, and to appoint special committees for specific functions or projects. The vice-president functions, in the absence of the president, in these same capacities. The secretary not only serves as the record keeper of the class for the benefit of the total Bible-school records program, she also will keep class minutes, write letters as directed, and contact absent class members to announce special class programs or activities. The treasurer will be responsible for special class funds raised for projects and socials. Committees are appointed by the president as needed.

Another method of organizing an adult class is the *group plan*. This does not eliminate the traditional class officers, but it does make the class organization revolve around groups and their captains. Under this plan, the class is divided into two groups. Each of these groups is led by a group captain who is responsible for his group's needs, attendance, etc. Combined with this group plan is a committee subplan composed of several standing committees. Every class member is a member of one of these committees. Such committees as visitation, social and recreational, stewardship, and project, could be set up.

The Size of the Class

Many feel the adult Bible-school class will function best when it is made up of thirty students or less. Whenever a class becomes larger than this, it is divided so that more effective teaching can be accomplished.

This suggestion may go against the tradition of many existing Bible schools, for many schools in the past have promoted the "large class" idea. However, the trend now seems to be away from large classes to smaller classes. Some points in favor of the smaller class are:

1. A smaller class provides a better student-teacher ratio. If the teacher is to effectively teach the truth of God to each student, he must know rather intimately each of his class members.

2. A smaller class provides more job opportunities. If the class is organized effectively, many more people can be involved in an active way with the class program.

3. The smaller class provides a better context for using a variety of teaching methods. Undoubtedly, large classes have contributed to the almost universal use of the lecture method in adult Christian education. After all, what else can you do effectively when you have a class membership of one hundred adults? Smaller classes, on the other hand, can be involved in discussion methods of various kinds.

Organizing a Leadership Training Program

A definite phase of adult education is leadership training. A church concerned with providing leaders for every phase of its program should have a continual training program. This can be accomplished only by an organized program of leadership training. These classes should be made available to all interested adults, but prospective teachers and leaders should be specifically recruited for them. Content courses in Bible, Christian doctrine, and church history should be supplemented with specific courses in the principles and techniques of teaching.

In order to have an effective training program there must be a careful planning of the curriculum. For example, a Primary teacher should be involved in learning experiences which relate to the nature and nurture of Primary children. Such a teacher also needs to be led to continually increase his or her knowledge of the Bible. Such a comprehensive program will be impossible without a well-organized plan of leadership training.

To supplement the basic leadership classes offered through the Adult Department, teachers and leaders should be encouraged to attend area clinics and conferences where special training may be received.

The time at which leadership classes should be scheduled will vary depending upon the community, and the size and the customs of the local congregation. Some may find it best to incorporate such classes into the Sunday-morning study hour, while others may prefer to have them on Sunday evening or some evening during the week.

Remember, leadership training is not a "mass" experience. Smaller classes of dedicated people meeting on a regular basis will do more for the church than attempting to get a majority of the church membership involved in some kind of a leadership study.

Books for Further Study

FLAKE, ARTHUR. *Sunday School Officers and Their Work*. Nashville: Convention Press.

GWYNN, PRICE H., JR. *Leadership Education in the Local Church*. Philadelphia: Westminster Press, 1952.

LAMBDIN, J. E. *Building a Church Training Program*. Nashville: Convention Press.

McKIBBEN, FRANK M. *Guiding Workers in Christian Education*. New York: Abingdon Press, 1953.

MURCH, JAMES DEFOREST. *Christian Education and the Local Church* (rev. ed.). Cincinnati: Standard Publishing, 1958.

WESTPHAL, EDWARD P. *The Church's Opportunity in Adult Education*. Philadelphia: Westminster Press.

Questions for Discussion

1. Give in your own words a definition of organization.

2. What are the four guidelines for organization suggested by Mr. Murch?

3. Survey the Adult Department of your local church and explain the system used for grading. How could it be improved?

4. What are the duties of a general superintendent in connection with the Adult Department in a small school?

5. Explain the group plan of organization for an adult class.

6. What are some of the disadvantages of a large adult class?

7. Why should we organize the leadership training program as a part of the Adult Department?

NOTES

[1] James DeForest Murch, *Christian Education and the Local Church* (rev. ed.; Cincinnati: Standard Publishing, 1958), p. 163.

CHAPTER 11

Counseling Adults

Introduction

Counseling and education. Counseling and education are closely related. They both involve problem solving and they both have the effecting of desirable changes as their goal. Harold Rutledge says that "counseling is an educational means in that it affords opportunity for the individual to learn about himself, thereby setting off an educational and growth chain reaction in which he learns about and better relates himself to his own small group, his family, his church, society and God." [1] Since this relationship is apparent, it is essential that some attention be given to counseling in a discussion of Christian education for adults.

A second look at counseling. It is imperative, for the purposes designed in this chapter, to recognize that counseling can be understood in a general sense rather than from a purely professional perspective. The professional aspects are not to be denied, but too often they are so emphasized that ordinary people are afraid to involve themselves in any way with other people if such involvement may appear to be a "counseling relationship." This ought not to be! The average adult Christian may often be as helpful in "preventive" counseling as the professional, because of his availability. Church leaders in the adult program of the church may be sought out more frequently for counseling (or "talk" as it often is termed) than a professional "minister" or "counselor." The teacher in the Adult Department may render a real ministry as a counselor.

Dr. A. Donald Bell[2] points out that, generally, "lay" people are in good communication with each other. He adds that people will come to group leaders rather than to some professional because (1) they may have built up psychological walls against clergymen or professional counselors, (2) the group leader's position is more permanent, or (3) the group leader is one who is in a respected position outside of the church. Whatever the reason, responsible leaders within the church need to be sensitive to these opportunities and try to develop a "helping" relationship that will involve friendship, understanding, and acceptance.

But counseling needs to be seen as a team effort. The average Christian, the church leader, and the vocational worker are all involved. Often problems can be seen by others, and the ones facing the problem encouraged to find help from others. Frequently, these problems will be of such nature that professional help will be needed. The church has an ally in the mental health movement and its practitioners. Both the mental health movement and the church look toward a common goal—the prevention of mental illness and the development of the optimal mental health potential and personal growth of each individual. Social workers, clinical psychologists, school counselors and psychiatrists must be seen as those who may be of help in the counseling program of the church. Local leaders need to know those symptoms of extreme conflict and severe emotional stress so that referral can be made and counsel can be given to families to seek professional help.[3]

A warning needs to be given at this point. In seeking professional help, the Christian family needs to have some guide by which they may determine whether the "professional" is really competent. Dr. Oates gives these seven tests, which could be used as a guide in such an evaluation:[4]

1. Who sponsors your counselor?
2. Has the person been in the community very long?
3. Has the person been adequately trained for his task?
4. Is the counselor a person of basic spiritual integrity?
5. Has the counselor been reasonably successful in dealing with other people's problems?
6. Does this person promise much and do little, or does he promise little and do much?
7. Can you trust this person basically?

Principles of Counseling

Though there is always the danger of oversimplification when discussing counseling, some general purposes can be set forth as guidelines for procedure at whatever level counseling may be done.

1. *First, and foremost, we help people to help themselves.* Counseling of every type has this as its basic purpose. Counseling that tends to make people dependent upon the counselor, or attempts to give advice, or has ready-made answers and solutions for all questions and problems is a caricature of true counseling and stands in opposition to basic Biblical principles. Counseling is always a "helping ministry" and is concerned with developing independent, responsible individuals.

2. *Counseling also should let in light.* Frequently, problem areas in adult lives are results of ignorance. Counseling can provide

resources and information to dispel this darkness. At this point, Bible study, an adequate church library, and general Christian literature become valuable aids that the counselor uses.

3. *Counseling should attempt to interpret feelings and attitudes.* If the counselor does nothing more than listen or provide a "sounding board" as people pour out their troubles or express their feelings, he can make a great contribution to peoples' lives.

4. *Counseling should always encourage self-reliance.* The only dependency that is justified is a dependency upon God as described in the Scripture. The counselor should strive to help Christian adults, depending upon God, cry out with Paul: "I can do all things through Christ which strengtheneth me" (Philippians 4:13). Good counseling attempts to help the individual develop this kind of humble self-reliance.

Techniques of Counseling

Although it would be impossible to give adequate attention to counseling techniques in this brief chapter, we shall point out some of them briefly.

1. *The atmosphere of acceptance must be set by the counselor.* The person in need must be recognized as a person who is important. It is an atmosphere that allows the needy person to talk about his problems without fear of shock, rejection, rebuke, or reprisal on the part of his counselor.

2. *The counselor must be capable of reflecting.* By this process the counselor attempts to mirror in different words the substance of the emotions or attitudes being expressed by the person in need. This not only reflects the feelings of the person but also becomes a means of providing insight for the person into his real problem.

3. *The counselor must be able to wait for the real problem.* This is important because frequently persons do not come to the real problem immediately. They may find it too painful to discuss. They may want to be sure the counselor appears competent, and that he will keep in confidence what they tell him. Sometimes they may not really know what their real problem is.

4. *Attentive listening is another important trait of the counselor.* Many people need only to "talk it out" with someone who can listen sympathetically. Any Christian adult ought to be able to provide this kind of help.

5. *The counselor must realize that pauses are significant.* The person who is listening needs to listen and not talk. If a long pause ensues, let it; usually the person with the problem will be helped more by silence than by a steady stream of conversation.

Clyde M. Narramore, in his book, *The Psychology of Counselling,* gives the following list of helps for the counsellor.[5]

1. Provide a place and atmosphere conducive to uninterrupted discussion.
2. Encourage the counselee to talk and express himself freely.
3. Reflect and restate what the counselee says, thereby encouraging him to clarify his own thoughts and to say more.
4. Do not register surprise at any information which the counselee reveals.
5. Refrain from censoring or judging what the counselee says.
6. Encourage the counselee to suggest and discuss his own possible solutions.
7. Maintain a confidential attitude toward all discussion.

Group Counseling

Although group life within the church does not exist primarily as a therapeutic or counseling tool, it can become such when properly guided. In fact, group therapy is becoming more and more popular in the general realm of counseling. Dr. John M. Price says:

> Organizations of the church, such as Sunday school and training programs, are readily usable in the counseling process. When discussion is employed in dealing with the information at hand, personality interchange naturally follows. A skillful leader will use this interchange to bring about personal growth. Discussion groups seek to bring about fellowship and personal interaction while dealing with some topic. Socials, young people's discussion periods, parents' meetings, and informal planning meetings within the organizational structure are examples. They will contain many possibilities for group dynamics and personal growth. [6]

In such groups, *group dynamics* may operate if properly guided. By group dynamics we mean an atmosphere in which acceptance is supreme, thus developing a group climate that encourages group members to share and contribute and that will bring about changes in the attitudes of the group members. This atmosphere will demand self-analysis and will contribute to the insight of each participant.[7]

Areas in Which Adults Need Counsel

Problems related to developmental tasks. Whenever adults fail to achieve the level of success society expects in their vocations, marriage, or emotional maturity, problems arise. These problems will be many and varied. Some will be minor, others major; some will build up such pressure as to destroy one's efficiency; others will be so isolated as to be inconsequential. Church leaders, however, need to be aware of these areas of conflict and try to give a helping hand to those in need.

Problems of marital adjustment. Perhaps the greatest area of potential conflict is marital adjustment. With young adults, premarital counseling can function as a preventive for such potential conflict. This can be done through the home and through the church, both in group counseling and individual counseling.[8]

What are some of the common causes of unhappiness in marriage? Research has shown that the following complaints are most frequently given: (1) Sexual maladjustment (is this a cause or a result?); (2) Conflict in the management of children; (3) Conflict over social activities; (4) Religion; (5) Differences over the management of income; (6) Problems of in-laws; (7) Problems involving mutual friends.[9]

Spiritual problems. Many sincere people in the church may seek help from a counselor regarding their relationship to their Lord. Concern about the validity of their conversion, forgiveness of sins committed, a weakness in yielding to certain temptations, and problems in understanding difficult Bible passages are some of the more common spiritual problems. Dealing with these problems will require a practical knowledge of the Scriptures and of theology.

Church problems. In the operation of the average church, problems may arise that will require consultation with a counselor. Such problems as personality conflicts, a change of ministers, changes in leadership responsibilities, or decisions regarding buildings and grounds can greatly disturb adults. Without the intervention of a wise counselor, adults may sometimes even be lost to the church.

The Goals of Counseling

We began this chapter by asserting that the goals of counseling and the goals of education are the same—the effecting of desirable changes in human life. Some of the desirable changes we want to bring about through the counseling of adults are stated in the following signs of emotional maturity stated by Dr. Leroy Garrett:[10]

1. *He is a person who dares to care.* This involves both the capacity and the courage to give and receive love. It implies a passionate commitment to others, not a withdrawal from the world of people and activity.

2. *He can come back after being hurt.* Maturity makes it possible for a person deeply hurt to still act like a gentleman and refrain from sulking, resentment, and blaming others. "Jesus taught us how to love in the face of hate and to hope in the face of despair. This is perhaps life's most difficult task, to love the unlovely and to hold out hope when all seems lost. The emotionally healthy person can do this because he realizes how completely com-

plex life is, how little he knows, and how much every man needs each other man." [11]

3. *He is a person who gains insight through involvement.* "The immature lives in a world of private reference and is insensitive to the needs of others." [12]

4. *He strives to be part of the answer rather than part of the problem.* In humility, he realizes that as a part of the human race, the problems and burdens of human life are partly his own. He resolves that he will act maturely in face of these problems and attempt to provide some help in their solution.

5. *He moves toward life.* He is life-affirming and has a reasonable optimism about man's predicament. He realizes that life is a struggle, but he believes man is equipped to win in the end. He will love people and enjoy being with others. Life-affirmation will mean adequate goals and a sense of direction. One can move toward life as either an extrovert or an introvert, and it is not necessary for one always to be on the go and doing something in order to be mentally healthy. One can be busy and still not move toward life. It is the attitude toward people and things that makes the difference. [13]

6. *He takes responsibility for his own actions and does not try to blame others.* To do otherwise is to be dishonest with oneself. One must see himself as he really is (at least, as much as possible) and develop a simplicity of character that "will bring a man to terms with himself."

7. *He can adequately evaluate himself.* To be honest with self must be joined by the desire to evaluate properly one's strengths and weaknesses. "There is no virtue in underselling one's self" just as there is no virtue in "thinking more highly" of one's self than one ought to think. "He will recognize that he, like all other people, has certain unacceptable desires and weaknesses, and though he knows some of these will always be present, he manages to live with himself, peacefully and to struggle toward greater maturity." [14]

8. *He has the ability to learn from experience.* Rigidity, prejudice, dogmatism, arbitrariness will be absent, for he knows that he may be wrong. He will be open to new discoveries and to fresh outbreaks of interpretative or applied truth.

9. *He will be adequately free from his group or culture.* He will maintain his own individuality and personhood in spite of group loyalty. He will never allow group relations to destroy his creativity and originality. Dr. Garrett says: "He has a degree of tolerance and appreciation of cultural differences. He is willing and able to inhibit those desires and practices tabooed by his culture,

and yet he will dare to be different if he thinks the situation demands it." [15]

10. *He develops the power of synthesis.* He is able to integrate human learning and experience so that life can be seen "steadily" and as a "whole." Through maturity "one learns to think and to act under pressure. He can draw upon his resources and refer to his frames of reference with the least awkwardness. He moves toward a more articulate way of life. He knows what he should do and so he moves steadily and gracefully in that direction." [16]

Conclusion

The church is the redemptive fellowship of Jesus Christ, who is not only Saviour and Lord but the Great Physician and healer. This redemptive community must minister mutually to its own needs. The mental, emotional, and spiritual health of its membership is of vital concern. The program of any local church must provide for such a ministry. This is the justification for a counseling ministry (and, for that matter, an educational ministry) in which adults are both "patients" and "practitioners," "helped" and "helpers." May each congregation make as adequate provision as it can for such a "healing and helping" ministry.

Books for Further Study

DRAKEFORD, JOHN W. *Counseling for Church Leaders.* Nashville: Broadman Press, 1961.

LANDIS, JUDSON and MARY. *Personal Adjustment, Marriage, and Family Living* (4th ed.). Englewood Cliffs, New Jersey: Prentice-Hall, Inc., 1965.

MACE, DAVID R. *What Is Marriage Counseling?* New York: Public Affairs Committee, 1957.

NARRAMORE, CLYDE M. *The Psychology of Counseling.* Grand Rapids: Zondervan Publishing House, 1962.

OATES, WAYNE E. *An Introduction to Pastoral Counseling.* Nashville: Broadman Press, 1959.

————. *Where to Go for Help.* Philadelphia: Westminster Press, 1957.

Questions for Discussion

1. Make a survey of the sources of counseling in your community and evaluate them in the light of the suggestions in this chapter.

2. How is counseling related to Christian education?

3. Name and explain three techniques of counseling.

4. Name four of the general areas in which adults are likely to need help from a counselor.

5. What teaching of the Bible can you cite that a counselor might use in dealing with some of the marriage problems mentioned in this chapter? (List the book, chapter, and verse.)

6. What is meant by the emotional maturity goal of developing the power of synthesis?

7. Discuss the importance of a counselor knowing when a person is in need of professional or psychiatric help.

8. Discuss the importance of the counselor keeping in confidence the problems of the counselee.

9. Discuss the importance of arranging the proper place and time for counsel.

NOTES

[1] Wayne E. Oates, "Pastoral Counseling and the Educational Ministry of the Church," *An Introduction to Pastoral Counseling* (Nashville: Broadman Press, 1959), p. 269. Used by permission.

[2] "The Counselor Training of Prospective Group Leaders," *ibid.*, pp. 298-300.

[3] Such works as Wayne E. Oates, *Where to Go for Help* (Philadelphia: Westminster Press, 1957), should be available.

[4] *Ibid.*, pp. 32-37.

[5] Clyde M. Narramore, *The Psychology of Counseling* (Grand Rapids: Zondervan Publishing House, 1962), p. 57. Used by permission.

[6] Wayne E. Oates, "The Processes of Group Counseling," *An Introduction to Pastoral Counseling* (Nashville: Broadman Press, 1959), p. 284. Used by permission.

[7] *Ibid.*, p. 277 ff.

[8] See Wayne E. Oates, *Premarital Pastoral Care and Counseling* (Nashville: Broadman Press, 1958).

[9] See Judson T. and Mary G. Landis, *Personal Adjustment, Marriage, and Family Living* (Englewood Cliffs, New Jersey: Prentice-Hall, Inc., 1950).

[10] "Toward Emotional Maturity," *Restoration Review*, Vol. I., No. 1 (Winter, 1959), pp. 41-46.

[11] Ibid., p. 43.

[12] *Ibid.*

[13] *Ibid.*, p. 44.

[14] *Ibid.*, p. 45.

[15] *Ibid.*, p. 46.

[16] *Ibid.*

CHAPTER 12

Adults and the Christian Home

A number of years ago, Dr. Henry F. Cope, said:

> No nobler social work, no deeper religious work, no higher educational work is done anywhere than that of the men and women, high or humble, who set themselves to the fitting of their children for life's business, equipping them with principles and habits upon which they may fall back in trying hours, and making them the sweetest, strongest, holiest, happiest place on earth.[1]

What Dr. Cope was emphasizing then still needs to be stressed—the family and the home environment are still very significant in Christian education. This area must not be neglected.

The Biblical Emphasis on the Home

The Bible has long maintained the importance of the family unit in the plan and purpose of God. In the patriarchal period of Biblical history, God worked through the family, the father, the patriarch, being the family representative with whom God dealt (cf. Genesis 12:1-3; 26:2-5; 35:1, 2; etc.). After the giving of the covenant to the nation of Israel at Sinai, the law, which directed the covenant life, made much of the family and its responsibility. Such basic laws as "Honour thy father and thy mother," and "Thou shalt not commit adultery," were enunciated to keep inviolate the purity and cohesiveness of the family unit. Other laws directed the families (the fathers, particularly) to instruct their children in the way of God. Following the specification of the "first and great commandment"—to love God with all the heart, soul, and might (Deuteronomy 6:5)—is another injunction for parents. Read Deuteronomy 6:6-9.

There are a number of practical admonitions for the family found in wisdom literature. Read Proverbs 1:8, 9; 3:1, 2; 4:1, 2, 5; 13:1; and 22:6.

There are a number of explicit references to family life in the Gospels which deserve our attention. Read John 19:26, 27; Mark 7:6-13; and Matthew 18:2-4, 5, 10.

Two key passages in understanding the relationships of members of the Christian family are Ephesians 5:22-33 and 6:1-4.

The family, then, is important, for God has so created it that it should be the very foundation of human society. Two "becoming one flesh" (Ephesians 5:31) and "being fruitful and multiplying" (Genesis 1:28)—to use Biblical phrases—is a humane necessity and the foundation of societal life. No culture can be found where family life is not a significant part of its structure.

Contrasts and Changes in the American Home

1. *Changes in the economic life.* Many contrasts and changes have taken place in the economic life of the American family. The family is no longer a productive team working at the same task as was true of rural America one hundred years ago. Now the family is organized economically around the father's job. This has produced differences in status, and it has changed the roles of the various members of the family. It has often led to both geographical and social mobility: geographical, in that there may be a change in the job opportunity or there may be a transfer of the father and family to another place; social, in that as advances and promotions are made social status is increased.

2. *Changes brought about by working mothers.* Working mothers are also more prevalent now. In 1890 only 13.9 percent of the total female working force were married and only a small number of those had children. By 1960 the number of married women in the working force was larger than that of single women, and the number of mothers had increased tremendously (from 1940 to 1950 the number of employed mothers increased by 350 percent).[2]

3. *Changes in family organization.* In the past, the husband and father was generally conceived of as the ultimate authority in the family circle. The traditional roles of mother and children were subordinate. In our day, the father has lost both authority and function and the "wife and children have come into places of greater power in decision making."[3] The wife and mother is better educated and has moved into a more flexible role than formerly. She more often is the one who disciplines, teaches, purchases, engages in community activities, and directs leisure activities.

As a result of this transition in family organization, there often develops problems of self-doubt, anxiety, and guilt on the part of both husband and wife. Frequently, boredom will also result and may motivate mutual infidelity. In some instances parental conflict in relation to children may be evidenced.

This change in family organization has affected the children of the family as well. In the past, children identified and gained status through the family and the family name. "Now a great part of his recognition (especially at adolescence) is achieved through accomplishment in school, community, and peer groups which compete strongly with the home for the time and loyalty of the child." [4]

4. *Changes in the educational system.* Another shift seen in family life that has produced a notable contrast to the past is the family's changing educational role. Aided by the state, which penalized noncompliance, education has been taken out of the family circle and transferred to educational institutions. This, undoubtedly, is inevitable in a culture where the need for specialized knowledge grows beyond what the average family can provide. Generally, this change has been hailed as a distinct advantage for both family and nation. Certain problems have arisen in this transition. One major problem is that of fostering religious heritage through the public schools.

5. *Changes in recreational habits.* It is surprising that, in the past two decades, the American people have been reclaiming the recreational function of the family. Studies have shown that "whereas in the third and fourth decades of this century, the trend was clearly for recreation to be dissociated from family life," more recently there has been "a self-conscious recovery of this function." [5] This is especially true in suburbia where middle-class families are more and more oriented to weekends when family activities, such as games, travel, and outings, are enjoyed together. It is rather strange that we are most concerned about families that "play together" but not too concerned about families that "pray together."

6. *Changes in concepts about sex and marriage.* Another contrast that is seen in present-day family life is the new concept of sex and marriage that now seems to prevail. This has given rise to a new sex morality which has undermined both the Biblical standards and the ethical standards held by a past generation. Premarital sexual relations and promiscuous extramarital relations have increased as the fears of detection, infection, and conception have been removed by technological advances in medicine and birth control. The causes of this change in sexual behavior and understanding are many and varied. Such matters as the "breakdown of small-community social controls; the weakening of religiously grounded sex ethics; the use of the automobile which puts youth beyond the surveillance of adults; the ready availability of contraceptives; and the sex stimulation from mass media" [6] have certainly contributed to the present situation.

There has also been a paralleling transition in the idea of marriage. Marriage often takes place at a younger age and is often seen in an idealistic and romanticized light. Mate selection is made more and more on the basis of physical appearance or sexual attraction. The religious and social concepts of marriage that guided our parents have given way to a concept of marriage that is tentative, experimental, and individualistic.

7. *Changes in family tensions.* Divorce, separation, and desertion are major signs of family tensions. We live in a society that accepts such as common and justifiable. Margaret Mead, the noted anthropologist, writes that "the most serious thing that is happening in the United States is that people enter marriage with the idea it is terminable."[7] These terminations are not to be found in any one social class but are prevalent in all classes at present. Studies have indicated that marital instability as seen among those marrying under 18 years of age (or at an unusually advanced age), generally develops in the first three years of marriage, is most likely to develop in a childless home, and tends to develop where the partners have themselves come from unhappy homes and childhood. Other factors as premarital pregnancy, shorter engagements, and courtship conflict are associated with a higher divorce rate.[8]

Of course family tensions do not always produce broken homes. There may be any number of "sick marriages" that will not eventuate in separation or divorce. It is important that more effective preparation for marriage be made and some help be given to those who are married so that good marital adjustment may result. Certainly the church can provide such help, for studies indicate that "happiness in marriage seems generally to be positively correlated with fairly steady church attendance for both partners at the same church."[9]

Teaching Religion in the Home

In light of the assessment of the status of current family life, and in obedience to the will of God as expressed in Scripture, Christian families (therefore, Christian adults) must accept the responsibility of teaching. We will find, as we accept this opportunity, a thrill and a challenge that will continually amaze us with the results accomplished and humble us as we recognize the wisdom and goodness of the living God, who is Father of us all.

The Home: a teaching institution. The following facts make the Christian home the ideal place to teach religion.[10]

1. *The child is completely environed by the home during the most impressionable years of his life.* More and more child psychologists are emphasizing the first four to six years of life as the formative period for human growth and development. What a great opportunity!

96

2. *The home can influence the child over an extended period of time.* The home is the dominant factor in the child's early life; in the early stages it is practically the only influence brought to bear. The home is not limited in time as is the Bible school or some other agency attempting to nurture child life.

3. *Teaching can be done in normal life situations in the home.* Most formal teaching, whether in public school or church school, is artificial, and, to that degree, somewhat ineffective. In the home, learning is natural and most effective.

4. *The home offers opportunities for repeated teaching and effective evaluation.* If repetition is a valid principle of education (and it is!), then the home provides for putting this principle into operation. It also provides opportunity to observe results and make evaluations of the effect of Christian teaching upon our children.

5. *The home provides the environment where the Christian religion can be "caught" as well as taught.* Parental example and the example of older children will be observed by the child. Attitudes and actions will be developed in light of this which is "caught." The desire for approval will lead children to develop those attitudes and courses of action desired by parents. (Of course, this assumes that parents will be consistently Christian in all that they say and do.)

6. *The home provides the "laboratory of life."* Here there is a variety of experiences in which parents have the opportunity to interpret the significance of the Christian faith for one's school life, one's studies, one's recreational life, and one's friends. Religion taught in and through the home would touch every area and every relationship in the child's experience.

7. *Above all, the home provides opportunity to deal with the child as an individual.* Individual relationships and applications are essential to good teaching.

Two Aspects of Family Education

As Christian parents realize their great opportunity for effective teaching, they should plan to make the most of this opportunity. Plans will include both formal and informal aspects of teaching.

Informal aspects will include the attempts to develop definite Christian attitudes by setting an example and a family atmosphere in which these can flourish. Love for God, fellowman, and family members will be *seen* as well as taught. Sincere respect by parents toward each other, toward children, toward others' property, toward authority will be reflected by children in the home. Proper sexual attitudes can be fostered informally by parents who are open and frank about childhood questions and who demonstrate sincere affection and conjugal love in the presence of their children. Other informal aspects as family worship, grace at meals, personal devotions at bedtime, and the provision of good Christian reading material should be included in the family education program.

Formal aspects of family education will include definite plans for parent-children interaction in which basic contents will be transmitted. Daily Bible reading and study (perhaps through a program of family worship) can be provided for older children. A program of reading Bible stories can be carried on for younger children. Teaching opportunities in the everyday experiences of homelife need to be sought constantly. Parents should cooperate with the church school by utilizing the "take-home" materials and reviewing each Sunday's lessons with their children.

Church-Home Cooperation in Christian Education

The Christian family does not stand alone; the church should aid and encourage each family to provide Christian nurture for its child life. To do this the church will be involved in a total program of education that will include a ministry to its families. This program (or ministry) of church-home education lays exacting demands on Christian adults, for they must provide not only the nurture of the child in the church school, but also at home. To do this demands that they become competent educators themselves.

A total program of church-family education must be built upon certain objectives, consciously conceived of as goals to be achieved. The following objectives are suggested:

1. The church should educate persons for Christian marriage and family living.

2. The church should establish a program of church-home cooperation.

3. The church should build and provide resources for family living and nurture.

4. The church should provide pastoral care for families.

5. The church should provide formal Christian nurture for every member of the family.

Dr. Lee J. Gable says: *"The local church should purpose, therefore, to guide the religious living of the family as a whole.* This guidance is best effected by an educational procedure. This procedure necessitates a program."[11]

What is involved in a program projected to achieve the above objectives? The following plans are suggested for consideration.

98

1. *Through its leadership, the local church should provide definite pastoral care for its families.* The elders, through a "shepherding plan," can relate the church's ministry to the needs of every family affiliated with the local church. Others besides the elders should be involved in "home visitation." Teachers, Cradle Roll visitors, and Home and Extension Department workers should visit regularly in the homes of those involved in their particular responsibilities. In this manner, the needs of new parents, shut-ins, invalids, and those in various institutions, and children and adults regularly attending Bible-school classes can be discovered and met. An understanding of the home situation will also provide better rapport between teacher and student. By such visitation the local church will be seen in the community as a concerned fellowship.

2. *The local church should provide general resources for family living and nurture through its library.* Books, pamphlets, and tracts relating to homelife can be placed in homes by the church, and Christian parents can be encouraged to subscribe to various publications that will provide needed help in family nurture.

3. *Special educational features should be provided from time to time in which family problems will be highlighted.* Checklists of such problems can be circulated (see end of chapter) upon which adults can indicate their interest, and a series of studies on those problems most frequently checked set up for Wednesday or Sunday evenings.

4. *Parents' study clubs could be formed, graded according to age and interests,* that could meet regularly (perhaps monthly or even more frequently) for study and discussion of common family problems and needs. Church Extension Service of Golden, Colorado, some years ago, presented plans for such a study group that it called "Hearth and Horizon Club" (based on a statement by Elizabeth, Princess Bibesco: "The perfect marriage is a hearth and a horizon.")

5. *The local church could adapt the "public school-home cooperation" system.* It could hold *open house* for parents each year, so that parents could come to the rooms where their children are taught and could have equipment, procedures, etc., explained with a view to developing a more cooperative relationship between parents and teachers.

Parent-teacher meetings could be projected at least once each year (and preferably each quarter) so that lesson materials, take-home papers, etc., could be previewed or surveyed. At such meetings parents and teachers could openly discuss ways that each could help the other in the nurture of the children.

6. *A program of parent sponsors or class parents* (like room mothers in the public school) *could be inaugurated* with these parents being responsible for school-home relationships for a period of time (perhaps three to six months). Hart says:

There are many ways in which these class parents can make valuable contribution to the group and the church school. Whenever there is a class activity in which the teacher needs the cooperation of the parents, these helpers will be the ones she can call on for assistance. The class parents will be responsible for promoting good fellowship. They will perhaps invite all the other parents to their home, having the teacher as honor guest. Thus the group will have a chance to share experiences and to get acquainted with the teacher and each other. When problems arise, the teacher will have persons who understand to whom she can go for counsel and assistance.[12]

Once these class parents have served effectively they will never again be disinterested in the Bible-school program for their children.

7. *Reports cards could be used by the Bible school.* These could be sent to parents each quarter or each month. The report form could include (1) attendance, (2) punctuality, (3) statement as to the general attitude of the pupil, (4) an estimate as to the quality of his work, and (5) something as to his spirit of cooperation.[13] The report could be so designed that parents could write back to the teacher indicating special problems or other items that the teacher should know in order to work with the student in a more fruitful way.

As we have noted above, these are all suggestions that could be used depending upon the needs and nature of each local congregation. We must always remember, however, that it is not by multiplying activities and agencies that a family-centered church is created, but by the inculcation of an attitude and a desire that will undergird all planning and programming.

Conclusion

Family life is not an end in itself; it is to be developed for the purpose of achieving God's eternal purpose. The effective family becomes a proving ground for developing effective Christians who are willing and capable of witnessing to the world about them of Jesus Christ and His redemptive power. The family is to nurture, so that members of the family may witness. The family that does this effectively will itself be a witness to God's program for human life. Let us remember the key to a Christian home rests in the hands of its adult members.

CHECK LIST

The Christian Answer to Family Problems

_____ 1. How Christian Parents Live Happily Together
What can couples do to make love last? What about the budget, hobbies, similar interests, etc.?

_____ 2. How to Use Discipline in the Family
Methods of discipline and securing obedience.

_____ 3. How to Counsel With Our Children
Establishing confidence and willingness to share; problems such as allowances, use of time, choosing friends, accepting responsibilities in the home, etc.

_____ 4. How We Can Avoid Dating Problems
First dates, going steady, late hours, what young people expect of parents in regard to dating, bringing dates to meet the family, etc.

_____ 5. How to Keep My Juvenile From Being Delinquent
Building family unity, family outings and observance of special days together, making the family the center of life.

_____ 6. How to Help Our Children Choose Their Vocations
The need for vocational guidance, determining abilities and interests, job opportunities today.

_____ 7. How to Help Our Children Grow Spiritually
Answering children's questions about God, teaching children to pray, the parents' relationship to the church school, use of Bible-story books, etc.

_____ 8. How to Understand Why Children Act As They Do
Principles of child psychology, child development, etc.

_____ 9. How to Help Brothers and Sisters Live Happily Together
Accepting the new baby, sharing responsibility, respecting one another's rights.

_____ 10. How to Share Your Home With Older Adults
Parents, grandparents, and in-laws.

_____ 11. How to Feather the "Empty Nest"
Readjustments after the children have married and moved away, how to retire and enjoy it.

_____ 12. Your suggestions, please:

Check six subjects you would be interested in. Double check the ones in which you are especially interested.

☐ Please check here if you feel that you would make an effort to attend this series of Adult Forum meetings on these topics on Sunday evenings at 6:30 this fall. A Nursery will be provided.

Prepared by Gordon Schroeder, First Baptist Church, Lincoln, Nebraska. Source: Church Extension Service, Golden, Colorado.

Books for Further Study

COPE, H. F. *Religious Education in the Family.* Chicago: University of Chicago Press, 1915. Old, but still helpful.

CROUCH, W. PERRY. *Guidance for Christian Home Life.* Nashville: Convention Press.

DUVALL, EVELYN M., and HILL, REUBEN L. *When You Marry* (rev. ed.). New York: Association Press, 1962.

FAIRCHILD, ROY W., and WYNN, JOHN. *Families in the Church: A Protestant Survey.* New York: Association Press, 1961.

FALLOW, WESNER. *The Modern Parent and the Teaching Church.* New York: Macmillan Company, 1947.

GABLE, LEE J. *Encyclopedia for Church Group Leaders.* New York: Association Press, 1959. Chapter 10. "How Can Church and Home Work Together?"

HART, W. NEILL. *Home and Church Working Together.* New York: Abingdon Press, 1952.

KERR, CLARENCE W. *God's Pattern for the Home.* Los Angeles: Cowman Publications, Inc., 1953.

LEAVELL, MARTHA BOONE. *Building a Christian Home.* Nashville: Convention Press.

LIGON, ERNEST. *Their Future Is Now.* New York: Macmillan Company, 1945.

————. *A Greater Generation.* New York: Macmillan Company, 1948.

NARRAMORE, CLYDE M. *How to Tell Your Children About Sex.* Grand Rapids: Zondervan Publishing House, 1958.

SCUDDER, C. W. *The Family in Christian Perspective.* Nashville: Broadman Press, 1962.

TRUEBLOOD, ELTON AND PAULINE. *The Recovery of Family Life.* New York: Harper & Brothers, 1953.

WYNN, JOHN CHARLES. *How Christian Parents Face Family Problems.* Philadelphia: Westminster Press, 1955.

Questions for Discussion

1. Analyze family life as seen in your community. Does your analysis agree with that presented in this chapter? Try to arrive at the reason for any difference there might be.

2. Discuss the home as an educational institution. List ways in which you teach in your home, formally and informally.

3. Do you believe that sex education should be carried out in the home? Why? What are the problems of promoting sex education in church or public school?

4. Discuss parent-teacher cooperation and expectations. Do you agree with the lists included in this chapter? Why?

5. How can each family show evangelistic concern within its community?

6. Discuss the cooperation of your church families in bringing their children to church functions.

NOTES

[1] H. F. Cope, *Religious Education in the Family* (Chicago: University of Chicago Press, 1915), p. 8.

[2] Roy W. Fairchild and John Wynn, *Families in the Church: A Protestant Survey* (New York: Association Press, 1961), p. 25. Used by permission.

[3] *Ibid.*, p. 26.

[4] *Ibid.*, p. 31.

[5] *Ibid.*, p. 37.

[6] *Ibid.*, p. 38.

[7] *Ibid.*, p. 43.

[8] *Ibid.*, p. 42 ff.

[9] *Ibid.*, p. 43.

[10] Much of the following is condensed from Findley B. Edge, *Teaching for Results* (Nashville: Broadman Press, 1956), pp. 180-184.

[11] Lee J. Gable, ed., *Encyclopedia for Church Group Leaders* (New York: Association Press, 1959), p. 293. Used by permission.

[12] *Ibid.*, p. 308.

[13] John L. Lobingier, *The Better Church School* (Philadelphia: United Church Press, 1952), p. 86. Quoted by *ibid.*, p. 312.

CHAPTER 13

The Goals of Adult Education

Introduction

In recent years we have come to recognize the importance of purpose in education. Purpose calls attention to *aims, objectives,* or *goals.* These aims or objectives or goals may be comprehensive or they may be specific. They may relate to a single class session or the total educational program of the church. When these comprehensive goals are stated, they become, in effect, our philosophy of education.

Such objectives or goals serve five major purposes:

1. They give direction to the processes through which desirable changes are to be realized.

2. They give proper sequence to educational activities.

3. They provide a guide for desirable changes.

4. They guide the selection of materials for use in the effective carrying out of desirable activities.

5. They serve as measures of the effectiveness of the educational process.

How do we arrive at goals or objectives? Christian education is not merely secular education with a halo. If Christianity is distinct and unique, then the goals of educating persons in the Christian faith will be unique and distinct. The goals for Christian education are ultimately to be derived from the Bible and human need, *in that order.* The Bible alone presents the will of God, the nature of created beings, the purpose of God in redemption, the nature and purpose of the primitive Christian community, and the final destiny of the world and all within it. In the light of this truth and in view of our contemporary human needs the goals of Christian education are determined. The goals thus developed, according to Dr. James H. Chapman, should satisfy the following demands:

(1) They should dovetail into practical, daily life, (2) They should cover religious, social, and personal needs of the individual, (3) They should be true to the accepted revelation of divine truth, (4) They should be true to the best ideals of human experience, (5) They should mould changing society by the pattern of the society that wisdom decrees should exist.[1]

The History of Christian Education Goals

Since the beginning of Christian education, goals are apparent. They may not always have been stated, but they are there nevertheless. Studies such as Kent's *The Great Teachers of Judaism and Christianity* and Sherrill's *The Rise of Christian Education* point out the goals or objectives that are to be seen in the teaching activity of the apostolic and postapostolic church. Similar studies of the educational philosophy of Luther, Calvin, Wesley, Campbell, and other great religious leaders reveal the goals that they accepted though they may not have stated them as such. A study of the literature of the Sunday-school movement reveals that goals or objectives are to be found here as well, although these goals undoubtedly went through a number of changes.

A Statement of Christian Education Goals

It was not until 1929, however, that any conscious attention was given to the development of a statement of goals for Christian education. In that year, Paul H. Vieth, director of research of the International Council of Religious Education, completed a study of comprehensive objectives. This study was presented to the faculty of Yale University as a doctoral dissertation. Later it was edited and published by Harper under the title, *Objectives in Religious Education*. Though published in 1930, it still remains a definitive work in the field of religious educational goals.

Dr. Vieth arrived at seven comprehensive objectives in his study. To these an objective on the "Christian family" has been added. These have become the accepted goals of Christian education by the educational forces aligned with the Division of Christian Education of the National Council of Churches of Christ in America. They are as follows:

God	I. Christian education seeks to foster in grown persons a consciousness of *God* as a reality in human experience, and a sense of personal relationship to Him.
Jesus Christ	II. Christian education seeks to develop in growing persons such an understanding and application of the personality, life, and teachings of *Jesus* as will lead to experience of Him as Saviour and Lord, loyalty to Him and His cause, and will manifest itself in daily life and conduct.
Christlike character	III. Christian education seeks to foster in growing persons a progressive and continuous development of Christlike *character*.

Christian social order	IV. Christian education seeks to develop in growing persons the ability and disposition to participate in and contribute constructively to the building of a *social order* throughout the world, embodying the ideal of the Fatherhood of God and the brotherhood of man.
Churchmanship	V. Christian education seeks to develop in growing persons the ability and disposition to participate in the organized society of Christians—the *Church*.
Christian family	VI. Christian education seeks to develop in growing persons an appreciation of the meaning and importance of the *Christian family,* and the ability and disposition to participate in and contribute constructively to the life of this primary social group.
Christian life philosophy	VII. Christian education seeks to lead growing persons into a Christian interpretation of life and the universe; the ability to see in it God's purpose and plan; a *life philosophy* bent on this interpretation.
Bible and other materials	VIII. Christian education seeks to effect in growing persons the assimilation of the best religious experience of the race, preeminently that recorded in the Bible as effective guidance to present experience! [2]

Another Statement of Christian Education Goals

There are, of course, many Christian communions who are not represented by the National Council of Churches and for whom these goals are not acceptable, for theological as well as political reasons. The Southern Baptist Convention, for example, has set forth the objective of its educational program in a pamphlet entitled *Unto a Full Grown Man,* and in *The Curriculum Guide* edited each year by Clifton J. Allen and W. L. Howse. In *Unto a Full Grown Man* seven major objectives are stated and then related significantly to each age group. These seven are: (1) In relation to the Bible; (2) In relation to God; (3) In relation to Jesus; (4) In relation to the church; (5) In relation to self; (6) In relation to others; and (7) In relation to the home. In *The Curriculum Guide* a comprehensive statement of objectives of Christian teaching and training is given:

The overarching objective is to help persons become aware of God as revealed in Jesus Christ, respond to Him in a personal commitment of faith, strive to follow Him in the full meaning of Christian discipleship, live in conscious recognition of the guidance and power of the Holy Spirit, and grow toward Christian maturity.

Summary

1. *Christian conversion*—To lead each person to a genuine experience of the forgiving and saving grace of God through Jesus Christ.

2. *Church membership*—To guide each Christian into intelligent, active, and devoted membership in a New Testament church.

3. *Christian worship*—To help each person to make Christian worship a vital and constant part of his expanding experience.

4. *Christian knowledge and conviction*—To help each person to grow toward mature Christian knowledge, understanding, and conviction.

5. *Christian attitudes and appreciations*—To assist each person in developing such Christian attitudes and appreciations that he will have a Christian approach to all of life.

6. *Christian living*—To guide each person in developing habits and skills which promote spiritual growth and in applying Christian standards of conduct in every area of life.

7. *Christian service*—To lead each person to invest his talents and skills in Christian service.[3]

Murch's Statement of Christian Education Goals

Other statements of objectives or goals could be listed, but one other viewpoint must suffice. James DeForest Murch's book, *Christian Education and the Local Church,* has long been a standard for evangelical Christians. This book has been frequently quoted and referred to in the past few years. His viewpoint in regard to the purpose of Christian education has been accepted widely. For example, the Committee on Philosophy and Practice of Christian Education of the National Association of Evangelicals (an interdenominational service agency) which published a definitive work in 1951 entitled *Christian Education in a Democracy,* under the general editorship of Dr. Frank E. Gaebelein, relies heavily upon Dr. Murch's views in this statement:

As to purpose, evangelicals hold that the main objective . . . is not just to construct a new social order, acquire Bible knowledge, or to strengthen and perpetuate institutional Christianity. Christ's purpose during his earthly ministry was to save men and to fit them to live in harmony with the will of God. When he gave his marching orders to the church he made it clear that her purpose was to be coextensive with his . . . If the Sunday School has a divine prerogative, it is to lead youth to a vital experience of Christ and to teach and train them to live in harmony with the will of God.[4]

Dr. Murch maintains that the ultimate goal of Christian education is "fitting men to live in perfect harmony with the will of God."[5] When we accept this goal, it provides us a practical vantage point from which to evaluate the total Christian education program of the local congregation.

107

Principles for Adapting These Goals

Once comprehensive goals have been developed it is necessary to adapt them to the educational program of the local church. This process should proceed upon the following principles:

1. *The needs of adults.* Always in setting up a program of education we should ask ourselves the question, What are the needs of adults in our local church? Those needs discussed in chapters 3, 4, and 5 should be carefully analyzed. The program of adult education for each local church should reflect a desire to meet these needs.

2. *The interests of adults.* Adult interests must be kept in mind when attempting to develop an effective educational program for them. Children, occupation, social life, civic concern, and health are but a few of the interests that must be considered in setting up an adult education program.

3. *The development of adults.* Adults are expected to develop physically, mentally, and socially. Both society and the church have certain achievements which they expect of adults. If the goals of adult education are to be reached, these expected plateaus must be considered.

A Practical Application of These Goals

The following statements adapted from *Unto a Full Grown Man* help us to see the practical application of the goals discussed in this chapter.

1. *The Bible.* The Christian education of adults seeks to lead them to know, appreciate, and acknowledge the Bible as the authoritative and sufficient source of God's will; to achieve skill in personal study of the Bible and in the application of Biblical truth to daily life.

2. *God.* Christian education seeks to lead adults to recognize God as Creator and Lord of all life; to develop an awareness of God as a living personality; and to help create a personal relationship with Him.

3. *Jesus Christ.* Christian education seeks to lead adults to understand and appreciate the life and teachings of Jesus Christ; to find in Jesus God's ultimate revelation; and to surrender their lives in complete dedication to Jesus as Saviour and Lord.

4. *Church.* Christian education seeks to foster in adults an understanding of the nature and mission of the church which Christ established; to become a responsible member of the local congregation by supporting actively the total church program; and to serve Christ through His Church with increasing effectiveness.

5. *Self.* Christian education seeks to develop in adults an understanding of the sacredness of human personality; to engage in a conscious progressive growth in Christlikeness; to develop a concept of truth, life, and the universe in harmony with the Biblical revelation; to claim the presence, power, and

leadership of the Holy Spirit in daily living; to accept the full responsibility of the Christian stewardship of all their possessions; and to appreciate and use the best in their religious heritage, experience, and culture.

6. *Others.* Christian education seeks to develop in adults that disposition toward others which is unselfish and seeks to promote their welfare; first, by attempting to bring them to acknowledge Jesus as Saviour, and second, by working for a Christian society throughout the world.

7. *Home.* Christian education seeks to develop in adults an understanding of God's will for the home and the ability and disposition to build a Christian home and provide for the spiritual nurture of their children. [6]

Conclusion

At the beginning of this chapter we stated five major purposes that goals serve. In conclusion, let us now be more specific in pointing out how these goals really function in the educational task of the church. First, they serve as a standard by which the program of Christian education can be evaluated. Is our teaching and training program for adults really accomplishing what we would like for it to do? Are adults building Christian homes, participating in the life of the church, becoming more aware of their personal relation to God, and understanding more and more of God's will through their knowledge of the Bible?

Second, these goals are basic to setting up an effective Adult Department. If we propose that adults should know the Bible so that they may understand God's will, then our study materials must be derived in large part from the Bible. Other units of study must be given over to an understanding of the Christian home, to Christian doctrine, to an understanding of the Holy Spirit, and to a study of our religious heritage. Some opportunity must also be provided in the development of leadership skills if we want adults to become responsible Christians.

Finally, these goals provide guidance for the total program of adult education in the church. This means that even informal activities of adult church life should conform to these goals. Nothing ought to be fostered for adults through the church that will not help produce the desired changes indicated in our statement of goals.

It is granted that upgrading of the adult program may be a slow, laborious task; but it will be worth the effort. Let us never cease to seek to help men and women live in more perfect harmony with God's will!

Books for Further Study

ALLEN, CLIFTON, and HOWSE, W. L. (eds.). *Curriculum Guide 1961-62.* Nashville: Convention Press, 1961.

MILLER, RANDOLPH CRUMP. *The Clue to Christian Education.* New York: Charles Scribner's Sons, 1950.

MURCH, JAMES DEFOREST. *Christian Education and the Local Church* (rev. ed.). Cincinnati: Standard Publishing, 1958. Chapter 11.

PRICE, JOHN M., *et. al. A Survey of Religious Education* (2nd ed.). New York: Ronald Press Co., 1959.

Unto a Full Grown Man. Nashville: Sunday School Board of the Southern Baptist Convention, n.d.

VIETH, PAUL H. *Objectives in Religious Education.* New York: Harper & Brothers, 1930.

ZEIGLER, EARL F. *Christian Education of Adults.* Philadelphia: Westminster Press, 1958. Chapter IV.

Questions for Discussion

1. Name the five purposes good objectives serve in Christian education.

2. From what two sources do we derive our goals in Christian education?

3. Name the eight goals of Christian education set forth by the Division of Christian Education of the National Council of Churches of Christ in America.

4. Why can Dr. Murch's concept, that the goal of Christian education is to fit men to live in perfect harmony with the will of God, be considered as a summary of all other goals?

5. Why must the interest of adults be considered in setting up a Christian education program for them?

6. Discuss the manner in which the following things apply to the goals in Christian education: the Bible, the church, and the home.

7. Why should we work continually at the task of improving the Adult Department?

NOTES

[1] John M. Price, *et. al., A Survey of Religious Education* (New York: Ronald Press Co., 1940), p. 112.

[2] *Curriculum Guide for the Local Church* (Chicago: National Council of Churches, 1950), p. 9.

[3] Clifton J. Allen and W. L. Howse, eds., *Curriculum Guide 1961-62* (Nashville: Convention Press, 1961), pp. 14, 15. Used by permission.

[4] Frank E. Gaebelein, *Christian Education in a Democracy* (New York: Oxford University Press, Inc., 1951), p. 227. Used by permission.

[5] James DeForest Murch, *Christian Education and the Local Church* (rev. ed.; Cincinnati: Standard Publishing, 1958), p. 100.

[6] In *The Curriculum Guide* put out each year by Convention Press a breakdown of general goals into ways and means of achieving them is attempted. See p. 31 ff. for adults.